Brand Slam

The Ultimate Hit in the Game of Marketing

Frank Delano

Lebhar-Friedman Books

New York   Chicago   Los Angeles   London   Paris   Tokyo

© 2001 Frank Delano

Lebhar-Friedman Books
425 Park Avenue
New York, NY 10022

Published by Lebhar-Friedman Books
Lebhar-Friedman Books is a company of Lebhar-Friedman, Inc.

Printed in the United States of America

Library of Congress Cataloging-in-Publication Data
on file at the Library of Congress

ISBN: 0-86730-847-8

Visit our Web site at lfbooks.com

For information on volume discounts call 212-756-5248

CONTENTS

ACKNOWLEDGMENTS

This book would not have been possible without those great brand generals and captains who had the vision, courage, determination, and talent to achieve the ultimate hit in the game of business, which I have coined "Brand Slam."

I would like to thank my publisher, Geoffrey Golson, and Frank Scatoni, acquisitions editor, for believing in this work. And to the others at Lebhar-Friedman Books—Kristen Izurieta, Sue Moskowitz, and Shawn J. Rubel—who contributed to the book's copyediting, marketing, promotion, and production; my sincere thanks to all of you.

My deepest appreciation also goes to Jeri Drefs for providing me with a weekly flow of advertising and brand trade news. Thanks Jeri for all of your support, encouragement, and insightful comments on the manuscript's first draft.

This book is dedicated to my best friend, Cosmos—a truly exceptional and handsome male golden retriever with a heart of gold. It's true when they say, "If you have only one loyal friend in your life, you're a lucky person."

INTRODUCTION

Enough with strategies, strategies, and more strategies. Ball games are won when a player steps up to the plate and smacks one out of the ball park. There's no strategy for that, just the human instinct to win.

A "grand slam" is the ultimate hit a player can achieve in the game of baseball. In the game of business, a "brand slam" is the ultimate feat a company can achieve at a moment of time in its history. It's that big hit that can catapult a new-economy brand to global marketing stardom, or transform an average old-economy brand into a colossal success overnight.

This book is about brand slams and those exceptional companies and individuals who have hit them. It's about achieving "WOW," which means delivering a devastating blow to your company's competitors. It reveals the *brilliance, inspiration,* and *business environment* that can lead to a brand slam. It highlights the leaders and looks at the *execution* of successful brand marketing. These are the *people* who helped separate their companies and products from the rest of the pack.

Going for a brand slam is no easy task. Often management must risk time, effort, money, and reputation to score that incredible brand slam.

My goal in writing this book was to provide the knowledge and insight needed for you to achieve a brand slam in your company. With that in mind, I have linked success stories to create an overarching view of the brands that remain indelible images in our minds today. If nothing else, I hope this book proves that it takes visionaries to hit brand slams, not corporate tacticians who spend their time writing 300-page strategic-brand plans that lack what I call a "big idea."

There's no better time to focus on brand marketing. Consumers' awareness and loyalty to your flagship brands are more important today than at any other time in your company's history. Thanks to the Internet, the image power once enjoyed by well-known consumer product brands such as Heinz, Hershey's, Campbell's, Kraft, Kellogg's, Ralston-Purina, Quaker Oats, Clorox, Hellmann's, Budweiser, RCA, Kodak, Colgate, and Gillette has diminished in recent years. Why? As millions of consumers surf the Net each day, they find a plethora of alternative—and often less-expensive—products and brands. They also see the advantages of competitor services and products. It's information that wasn't so readily available to consumers prior to the explosive growth of the World Wide Web in 1998.

Just as the emergence of the shopping mall was a devastating blow to mom-and-pop retail stores in the 1950s, the Internet has changed the way people shop today. Now it's the shopping malls that are feeling the pressure of decreased sales performance. Why fight traffic or deal with nasty weather when you can simply log on to a shopping extravaganza. In the comfort of your own home, you can order any item you want with the click of a button and a major credit card. Consider the millions of dollars in sales that Beauty.com, Sports.com, and Shop@aol.com have taken from retail stores in malls across America since their debut in the late 1990s. The challenge here—even for dot-coms—is for a company to *not* rest on its laurels and to be an innovative trendsetter.

After reading this book, you will know what it means to hit a brand slam. Brand slams come in many forms, shapes, and sizes. Take Pfizer's Viagra impotence pill. Just one month after its introduction in April 1998, this product has become part of the world's vernacular regardless of the language spoken. Another brand slam: "Please don't squeeze the Charmin!" This big idea for an advertising campaign is so compelling and memorable that it has forever etched the Charmin brand and the product's TV spokesman, Mr. Whipple, in our minds. And what about the return of an old classic like the Volkswagen Beetle in a new heart-throbbing aerodynamic design? Or the hit TV game show, *Who Wants to Be a Millionaire?* Thanks to the show's popular host, Regis Philbin, the phrase "Is that your final answer?" jumped into corporate boardrooms and homes across America. The list is endless.

Rarely do we see a brand slam every day, every week, or every month. But when it does happen, it's contagious. It captures the attention of the public and the media in much the same way that a blockbuster movie like *Titanic* captures the hearts of moviegoers everywhere. Everyone has to see the movie or buy the product. How many new brand-name products get a full hour on CNN's *Larry King Live?* Viagra did. Now that's what I call a brand slam.

The book also covers some of the most memorable advertising themes of the twentieth century. Remember Apple's "1984"; Wendy's "Where's the beef?"; Diet Coke's "Just for the taste of it"; L'Oréal's "I'm worth it"; and McDonald's "You deserve a break today"? When you hit an advertising brand slam, the ad's theme line and the product's image are unforgettable.

If the book's title *Brand Slam* got your attention, that's precisely what it was intended to do. But in truth, I coined the phrase *brand slam* to show that successful brand marketing requires a team effort. Everyone directly or indirectly involved in building a company's brand should focus on creating WOW. Let's face it, if your company's brands are not creating WOW—whether it be in TV commercials and print ads, in product catalogues, on retailer shelves, in dealer showrooms, or on the Internet—your company may not be around long.

In *Brand Slam*, there's no step-by-step process for building a great brand. Even if such a methodology existed, it could not be applied across the board to every company and every industry. Nor is this book focused on long-term strategic brand management. It's about *brilliant marketing* and *product ideas* that come to fruition through people—people with incredible talent, energy, and a relentless desire to achieve WOW. It's about brand slams, which are one-time events that knock the socks off a company's competitors. It's brand marketing so awesome that it captures the public and the media's attention for months, even years; it's "the fabric of our lives."

Most books published on building brands are simply about strategies. If not, they are about brand positioning or managing brand equity. The overriding theme of *Brand Slam* is that it takes a *big idea*, not strategies devised by tacticians, to hit a brand slam for a new product, service experience, or business venture.

TIME FOR A CHANGE

On March 8, 2000, Procter & Gamble's stock price plummeted 27 percent, following news that the company predicted weaker than expected earnings in the next quarter. How does the undisputed king of consumer brand-name products lose almost one-third of its market capitalization in one day?

Sears, Roebuck and Co., founded in 1886, is America's oldest one-stop shopping department store chain and a mammoth retailing operation. However, its market cap is only $10 billion in the strongest bull market in American history. Why is it that several dot-coms founded in the mid-1990s have a market cap greater than that of Sears? Some Wall Street gurus say it's because both P&G and Sears are seen as old-economy companies with slow-growing brands. Big-name dot-coms, on the other hand, are among the elite group of new-economy companies with fast-growing brands. That's the easy answer; I think there's more to it.

Many long-standing companies have spent the last three decades micromanaging their well-established brands. They have become masters of discount coupons and low-budget production, devising strategies to save a penny or two in the design, packaging, marketing, and distribution of their brand-name products. In contrast, the dot-coms are creating breakaway ideas that will forever change the way we do business and live our lives. Therein lies the true reason for the differences in market cap valuations. And here's the kicker: The dot-coms have convinced Wall Street and investors that a successful Internet company is entitled to report astronomical losses for four or five years—something unheard of in the history of the stock market. It's too early to tell how successful these new-economy businesses will be in the long term, but the fact remains that the Internet has forever changed the way we do business. And if some of the old standbys don't adapt accordingly, they may be gobbled up by the new lions in the business world.

It's time for old-economy consumer-brand companies to show consumers, Wall Street, and the media that they *still* have what it takes to hit brand slams. Remember, it was a brand slam product—not strategies—that helped make many formerly small, family-run businesses into manufacturing giants.

When H.J. Heinz was in England in 1876, he tasted a fish-based condiment called catsup. He liked the product's concept but felt the condiment would be more appetizing to Americans if tomatoes were the base ingredient. He returned the same year to the United States and developed a recipe for tomato catsup. In a matter of months, Heinz Catsup (known today as Heinz Tomato Ketchup) debuted. That single product's success was the foundation for a food empire that spans the globe today.

If your job has anything to do with building brands, I suggest you put this reminder note on your desk: *H.J. Heinz was not a brand caretaker, he was a brand maker.* If you don't grasp the difference, you'll never hit a brand slam.

Traveling one day on an elevated train, Heinz took notice of a sign on a building that read: "We have 21 styles of shoes." Within a few days he came up with Heinz 57 Varieties. It would become one of the most memorable brand slogans in the annals of American advertising. When Heinz instructed one of his managers to put the phrase "Heinz 57 Varieties" on every product label and factory sign, the manager reminded him that the Heinz company had more than 57 varieties. Heinz told him that people would remember the number 57. He was right. Heinz hit brand slam consumer products long before the light bulb and the telephone were fixtures in American homes.

A BRAND IS ANYTHING AND EVERYTHING

Brands encompass "anything" and "everything" in our lives. You are a brand by the very fact that your name and physical appearance differentiate you from billions of other people living on planet earth. Your brand's image is the perception of your personality, character, dependability, intelligence, job, social ranking, and behavior as held in the minds of your friends, peers, and neighbors. Your home is a brand. Your home's street address, the name of the town or city where you live, the name of the county, state, and region where you live, and the country where you live all are brands. The 1998 Oscar-winning picture *Shakespeare in Love,* the New York Yankees, the Statue of Liberty, Saint Patrick's Cathedral, the Visiting Nurse Services of New York, the New Hampshire Primary Elections, CNN, and musical artist Carlos Santana are brands, too. They're just a little different from the traditional consumer products that we've all come to know—brands like Cheer liquid detergent, Huggies baby wipes, and Diet Pepsi.

So why is it that the vast majority of companies that manufacture or market brand-name products never seem to hit a brand slam? It's not because they don't want to. In most cases, it's because management holds the reins too tight on its brands and is unwilling to venture into new territory. Again, my goal in writing this book is to offer you, the reader, insight on how to hit a brand slam, and to provide lessons from the marketplace on how your company (even if it's a nonprofit organization) can go for that ultimate brand slam that will set you apart from the competition.

NEW ECONOMY OR OLD, IT'S STILL ABOUT BRANDS

As the new century rolled in, "old-economy" and "new-economy" brands became hot buzzwords for Wall Street pros and the world's media. Let's not forget that a brand is a brand no matter who cut the cloth. Everyone buys based on a brand. It's irrelevant if that brand dates back to the Civil War or if it's today's new dot-com. "Old brands" have withstood the test of time and are far from being over-the-hill. Every time shock waves hit the Nasdaq stock market, investors flee to those NYSE-listed old-economy companies with time-tested brands.

THE RIGHT TECHNOLOGY MAKES A DIFFERENCE

Not that long ago, computers were the size of a home refrigerator. Then they shrank to the size of a Coleman cooler. Now you can find computers the size of a notebook pad, and experts predict that by 2005, you'll be able to wear a PC on your wrist. Compare that to the 1949 issue of *Popular Mechanics,* which predicted: "Computers in the future may weigh no more than 1.5 tons." Try carrying that one on your wrist!

When I first heard about email in 1995, I was among skeptics who said that the Internet will eventually disconnect us from personalized communications. I was wrong. I send more email letters to acquaintances in Europe, South America, and Australia in a month than I sent in the previous two decades through "snail mail." Best of all, I don't have to deal with international postage and airmail stationery. One hundred years ago, people communicated to each other by a post-delivered handwritten letter. Then the telephone revolutionized the way people communicated with each other. Now, millions of people are finding that sending email is easier and more cost-effective than making phone calls.

Internet technology connects us with people around the world, and consumers are starting to change the way they make purchases and how they find entertainment at home. I agree with Steve Case, America Online's chairman and CEO, that the future is in connecting the PC, TV, and telephone in one seamless way. Two years from now it will be as easy to go online and buy shares of a German company as it is to buy an American company's stock today. The job of stock broker is now on the endangered species list. The New York Stock Exchange's trading floor may even disappear as e-stock trading becomes the medium of choice for big institutional investors.

The Internet has changed the playing field of traditional brand marketing. It's taking the place of the grocery aisle and product catalogue. More important, it's influencing which brands are chosen most often and why. Yet, the Internet has given companies, old and new, around the world more opportunities to hit a brand slam than at any other time in history.

1

FIRST CREATE "WOW"— BRAND STRATEGY COMES LATER

"Whether you've eaten in a café restaurant or a three-star Michelin restaurant, it's all about coming away and saying 'WOW.'"

Oscar-winning actor Robert Duval

Too many old-economy companies suffer from a marketing disease that I call "strategitis." A primary symptom of this disease is an uncontrollable compulsion to develop brand strategies that are missing a big product idea. In contrast, new-economy companies are all about developing big product ideas. When they hit on one that ignites their e-charged engines, they move like the speed of email to transform that idea into a tangible e-commerce product. That's why new-economy companies have gobbled up most of the $25 billion in Internet sales for the year 2000.[1]

When a company's chief brand officer tells me that their first order of business is to develop a brand strategy, here's what I say: "What you need to create first is WOW—the brand strategy to launch WOW comes later." Without a new product or business venture with WOW excitement, you'll end up with a brand plan that's about as exciting as eating a slice of Wonder bread. Unless you have incredible toppings to spice it up, you could be facing a costly product or business venture failure.

---

1. Source: Gartner Group.

The musical *Big* is on the list of the shortest running Broadway shows of all time. The movie *Big* with Tom Hanks was a box office hit, but the adaptation to a live stage performance failed. Critics and the show's audiences found the live production lacking a WOW cast, which resulted in a lackluster performance. Andrew Lloyd Webber's musical *Cats*, on the other hand, holds the record for the longest-running show on Broadway—seventeen years! *Cats* delivered WOW performances to audiences night after night, and matinee after matinee.

Famous brand-name retail stores including B. Altman's, Bonwit Teller, Gimbel's, Abraham & Strauss, John Wanamaker, Montgomery Ward, Korvettes, Alexander's, and Woolworth are all gone. They simply ran out of WOW. Meanwhile, Ralph Lauren and Polo brand stores, now numbering more than one hundred in America and overseas, are racking up billions of dollars in sales. Why? If you're looking for designer menswear and fragrances, sleepwear, bath towels, footwear, underwear, hosiery, hats, scarves, handbags, luggage, sunglasses, jewelry, watches, furniture, and even wall paint—Ralph Lauren delivers WOW. There's nothing that the designer Lauren does that's second-rate or boring to the eye. Therein lies his marketing genius. Paying attention to product design and manufacturing details, keeping his stores in pristine condition, and recruiting the brightest people in the retail business are all factors that separate the Ralph Lauren brand from the pack.

Dodge's Dynasty, Chrysler's Eagle Talon, Ford's Aspire, Oldsmobile's Calais, and Cadillac's Cimarron all bombed because they had no WOW appeal in terms of design styling, engineering, and road handling performance to lure target buyers. On the other hand, Toyota's Camry, Honda's Accord, and Ford's Taurus continue to be the best-selling cars in America year after year. The price value and the total design package of these family cars add up to WOW in the minds of buyers. It's that simple.

Priceline.com, founded by Jay Walker in 1995, aired a barrage of TV commercials in early 2000. Veteran *Star Trek* actor William Shatner, the pitch man in the spots, reminds us that everybody knows someone who is saving money with Priceline.com. The WOW first created by Priceline's ad campaign was based on a simple idea—give consumers the power, freedom, and control to decide the purchase price they're willing to pay for groceries, gasoline, airline tickets, hotel rooms, car rentals, home mortgages, and long-distance calls.

This once high-flying Internet stock has had a series of major setbacks, including the loss of supermarket and gasoline contracts, slowing airline ticket sales, unfavorable publicity over consumer complaints, and the departure of top executives. Priceline shares fell 97 percent in the year 2000, closing at $1-5/16 in Nasdaq trade as of December 29, 2000. Walker stepped down as vice chairman at year-end with an estimated $60 million stake in Priceline, a fraction of what his shares were worth when Priceline's stock soared to more than $150 in 1999.[2] The lesson here is that when you fail to deliver on your advertised promise, the WOW that you initially achieved is history.

Jeff Bezos, Amazon.com's founder, CEO, and chief strategist, did a TV interview after he appeared on the cover of *Time* magazine's "Man of the Year, 1999." He said that the idea to start a Web bookstore just came to him out of the blue while he was cruising along a Seattle highway. That idea made Bezos a billionaire. And in return, he's been hailed as the person who gave the world a vision of how the Internet could revolutionize the way consumers buy goods. NBC News reported that during the 2000 Christmas shopping season, Amazon.com received 31 million electronic consumer orders; 99 percent of those orders were delivered on time. That's almost double the orders Amazon.com received for the previous Christmas shopping season, and a vast improvement in on-time delivery.

Bezos started his e-commerce business out of his parents' garage in 1994, when the World Wide Web was emerging on the horizon, but still in its infancy. He realized that books could be shipped easily and that a Web bookstore could have a larger inventory than a typical "Main Street" book shop. Bezos also visualized other products in addition to books that would be easy to sell over the Web. In 1998, Amazon.com added music CDs to its Web site. Since then, toys, videos, vintage watches, art and collectibles, tools and hardware, and beauty and health products have been added to the Web menu list. Again, an idea to achieve WOW in selling products via the Internet came first, the business and brand marketing plan followed, and the rest is history.

Another big idea that brought forth the Internet revolution originated with Jerry Yang, cofounder of Yahoo! In 1994, when Yang was a Stanford University graduate student, he got the idea for a directory service to help people surf the Web. But the Yahoo! that Yang envisioned would not only be a Web search engine, it also would bring a sense of organization to the Web's extensive content.

What Yang and cofounder David Filo launched with $1 million in seed money has—as of April 2000—grown to a company with $70 billion in market capitalization. And for all the millions of people that surf the Net each day, Yahoo! is the gateway to cyberspace. With that brand perception, it's little wonder why the biggest advertisers look to Yahoo! as the vehicle to reach target buyers of their products. Yang was among the first of the new-economy brand makers to see the future in wireless communication. Today, you can access Yahoo! anywhere with a wireless phone.

Yang has built a powerhouse brand by making users feel they drive the Net and have more information at their fingertips than they would with competitors such as Excite and Lycos. Now that's WOW!

---

2. *Source of stock price data:* Reuters News Service, *December 29, 2000.*

AN OBSESSION WITH STRATEGIC BRAND PLANNING

Over the past twenty-five years of building brands for industry giants, I have found two styles of managing a company's brands. One is the entrepreneur—managers cut from the same cloth as the legendary brand maker H.J. Heinz who are always looking for inspiration and the opportunity to create WOW with a new product. The other is the brand caretaker—managers who like to manage people. The latter spend much of their workdays planning meetings with staff, ad agency people, and outside advisors. Some of these folks have been known to spend up to three years in the strategic-brand planning stages before getting the show on the road. While they're busy editing and rewriting sections in a 300-page brand plan report, their competitor's knock-your-socks-off new product debuts on ABC's *Good Morning America,* NBC's *Today* show, CNN News, and CNBC's *Power Lunch* segment.

Too much time spent writing and rewriting strategic brand plans leads to a condition called "new product constipation." The best remedy for that ailment is to start cranking out ideas for a brand slam product, and toss the unfinished "strategic brand plan" report in a waste bin.

In the 1980s, anything with the word *strategic* in front of it got the ear of management. Recently, I attended a meeting held by a major manufacturer. Looking at the business cards handed to me by the people seated around the conference table, I couldn't help but chuckle inside at their job titles. They included strategic general marketing director, strategic brand director, strategic new product manager, strategic consumer research director, strategic communications director, strategic director of strategic business strategies, strategic planning coordinator, strategic advertising manager, and strategic national sales director.

A card handed to me by one executive listed the woman's name as simply, "operations director." I looked at her and said, "Looks like you're the only one attending this session who's not a strategist with a strategy." She replied, "The reason we hired you, Frank, is because we don't have a strategist with a strategy."

No sooner did she finish when my brain kicked in: "Delano, you fool, you need to change your job title from CEO and creative head of Delano & Young to something more strategic-sounding." Then an idea hit me: How about "strategic supreme commander of strategic marketing forces for strategic brand strategies in strategic global markets"? I could hear Jay Leno on NBC's *Tonight* show saying, "Now, that's impressive!"

Of course, I'm being facetious. But the inanity of my example illustrates a point. Before you form a committee of twenty-five people to spend the next eighteen months developing and writing a strategic brand plan for a new product or business venture, take some advice from best-selling author John Irving. He knows how to turn his ideas into brand slam novels like *The*

Cider House Rules, which he also adapted for a screenplay. Irving received an Oscar at the 72nd Academy Awards for that brilliant work.

Are you ready for this? Irving writes the last lines of his novel first, before he develops a story line for the book. He believes that if the reader plows through 350 pages of printed text that there should be something waiting at the end to make the journey worthwhile.

When a client sends me a 300-page "strategic brand plan" report to review, I turn to the summary usually found at the end of the report. If the last paragraph reads, "In conclusion, this committee recommends to management that it allocates the necessary budget and human resources to develop a new product that will prove to be a marketing success with consumers when it's launched," the report is useless to me. That's because there's no product idea to evaluate.

What are the lessons here for new- and old-economy companies?

LESSONS LEARNED

1. "Big Ideas" that create WOW are simple and clear in concept.

2. Only use the word "strategic" when you can back it up with real substance.

3. Write down what you think will be the last lines of your "Brand Plan" report to management. If they don't sound like WOW to you, then focus your time and efforts on coming up with WOW before you write the report.

4. It's worth repeating again: Enough with the strategies, strategies, and more strategies. Ball games usually are won when a player steps up to the plate and smacks one over the outfield fence. There's no strategy for that, just the human instinct to win.

2

IT ALL STARTS
WITH A "BIG IDEA"

Every brand slam starts with a big idea. But for that idea to take root it has to be presented to management in such a convincing way that it changes from an intangible idea to a visual image that management can relate to.

A BIG IDEA CREATES A LASTING MONUMENT

No one will argue that one of the world's most cherished brand icons is the Statue of Liberty, which stands more than 300 feet tall on Liberty Island in New York City's harbor. At the time it was erected, it was the tallest structure on view in the Manhattan skyline. Yet, it wouldn't be standing there had it not been for a Frenchman. Overwhelmed with America's open democracy and its promise of freedom and liberty to all of its citizens, he proposed that the French government commission a monumental gift from the French people to the American people.

His idea was so convincing to the French political ruling party at the time, that master sculptor Frederic-Auguste Bartholdi looked to America and saw the perfect gift to celebrate America's Centennial, a "Lady of Liberty." That's what happens when the power of a big idea takes root.

HOW THE AMERICAN EXPRESS
BLUE SQUARE LOGO WAS BORN

Today, the American Express "blue square" ranks among the top five most recognized logos in the world. Travel anywhere around the globe and you'll see the blue square. No matter what language you speak, this graphic icon instantly says the American Express Card is welcome at this establishment.

Now, here's how the blue square logo came to be. The story underscores my point that a big idea is going nowhere unless you can sell it to a company's chairman, CEO, and president.

Back in the early 1970s, Lippincott & Margulies was retained by American Express to develop a new brand logo and graphic identity system. I was head of design at L&M at the time, and took creative responsibility for this major corporate identity project. The original American Express logo was a horizontal blue bar with the company's brand name appearing in black type inside the bar. A white outline tracing the letters separated the two colors. While the logo had many visual flaws, it was known by millions of people around the globe. Thinking about the brand equity established in this logo, an idea hit me with considerable impact—redesign the logo in such a way that it would be more contemporary, powerful, and memorable.

I didn't like the look of the words *American Express* stretched across the length of the horizontal bar. It reminded me of the name badge on a flight attendant's uniform. The horizontal bar logo looked weak next to the Visa, MasterCard, Diners Club, and Carte Blanche logos displayed on merchants' doors and windows.

I made dozens of photocopies of the bar logo. Then the process began of cutting and pasting together different geometrical and circular-like shapes. Remember, these were the days before desktop computers and digital scanners. About a week later, I had some fifty rough logo shapes tacked up on the design studio walls. The design that had the most impact on me and my staff featured the American Express name stacked and positioned optically in the middle of a solid blue square. There was no reason for the brand's name to be in the color black since the white outline around the letters separated the name from the background shape.

While we worked on the blue square design, we also developed other logo-design concepts. My goal was to have three finalist logo recommendations to present to American Express' management.

Howard Clarke was then chairman and CEO of American Express, and his heir apparent was James Robinson, III, then executive vice president. Clarke ruled the diversified financial-services giant like a five-star general. I learned weeks earlier that Clarke personally had a hand in designing the original American Express bar logo. That added to my belief that Clarke would like the new blue square design, since it was adapted from the company's founding logo.

Two months went by and we worked feverishly to put together a WOW presentation of our best designs. We designed and had printed a complete line of corporate stationery for each of the top three logos. We constructed three large wall-mounted signs featuring each finalist logo design in a recommended color. To help management evaluate each logo in a real-life setting, we printed decals of each design and affixed each on an actual merchant's glass door next to the logos of Visa, MasterCard, and other financial brand logos and symbols. This real-life test was photographed for a planned slide presentation of our top designs.

The day finally came to present our logo creations to management. The setting was in the boardroom at American Express' former downtown New York headquarters. Some twenty-five executives and representatives of the company's ad agency took their seats at a large horseshoe-shaped dark mahogany table that seemed to fill the entire room. I began the slide presentation. First I went through the criteria we followed in developing our designs. On the next slide, one hundred logo design ideas that we developed over the project's three month period were shown in sketch form. This supported my comment that we undertook a thorough logo design study. Then I presented our top three design recommendations. As each appeared in color on the screen, I spoke about the design's merits. I left the blue square logo on the screen. "This design ranks No. 1 among all the designs you've seen this afternoon," I said. "It bridges the company's past with its future aspirations. It will become one of the most memorable logo designs ever created for an American company. Now, it's time to hear from you."

I looked at Clarke and Robinson who were seated at the far end of the table and received no positive or negative body language from either of them. It seemed like minutes before someone finally spoke up. The following comments, while not verbatim, are just a few that I recall hearing from those who attended the design presentation.

> "I don't like any of these designs."

> "I am disappointed with the logos you developed."

> "We thought we were hiring the best talent in New York, and you come in here and have the nerve to present these designs."

As each negative comment was voiced, it only invited another negative comment from someone else. Then I noticed Clarke whispering something in Robinson's ear. Robinson turned to his right and said something to the person seated next to him. That person turned to his right and said something to the person next to him. Suddenly everyone was whispering, and I couldn't hear a word that was being said.

As I was thinking of what I could possibly say to reverse this unexpected tidal wave of negativity for the blue square logo, some twenty people rose to their feet and began applauding.

"It's a brilliant logo design, a masterpiece," declared one executive.

"Frank, you did a remarkable job," stated another person.

"How soon can we reproduce the art of this great logo design. I can't wait to get this logo into our new ad campaign," said an ad agency executive.

One by one they came over to shake my hand. I learned later that Clarke told Robinson that he loved the blue square design.

Never underestimate the power of a company's chairman and CEO!

A BIG IDEA NEEDS A BRAND SLAM PRESENTATION

To sell a big idea requires visualization of that idea. And nothing beats the power of a three-dimensional model of the new product concept. Many big ideas have stalled because brand managers aren't given the freedom and budgets they need to put together a WOW presentation of their concept to management. Spending $1 million to bring to life a big idea is pocket change for some companies, when you consider that a new brand slam product rolled out nationally could rack up $1 billion in sales over the next five or ten years.

Let's look at the $7.7 billion cereal business.[1] Brand managers responsible for launching a new cereal product have asked me: "You've created brand names for so many products, why is it that you've never named a breakfast cereal?" I tell them it's because cereal brand managers have bite-size budgets and usually no budget for creating a WOW presentation. If you're a New York-based brand specialist firm, like we are, a $10,000 cap to develop brand-name ideas for a new breakfast cereal product buys only a few crunchy bites. And that's not going to satisfy a brand manager's hungry appetite for breakaway brand-name ideas. Such unrealistic and low-budget naming projects typically are assumed by freelance writers who have never named a major consumer product before and have no experience in clearing names for international trademark availability. Very often, these brand managers end up hiring five or six freelancers before they arrive at a short list of names to present to management. Then comes the shocking news that after spending $50,000, none of the names on the short list are available for the branding of a grocery product. Even worse, you may end up with a "misery" brand name. A "misery" brand name is a phonetically imperfect name or inappropriate image name. Consider Kraft Foods' new Post Cinna-Cluster Raisin Bran as a prime example.

---

1. Source: *Information Resources Inc.*

The cereal category hasn't seen a lot of growth, and the people at Post cereals wanted to offer consumers a new cereal that instantly appealed to their taste satisfaction. According to Post, cinnamon is consumers' third-favorite spice, and many cinnamon-flavored products are up in sales in the breakfast-food categories.[2] But here's the problem with the Cinna-Cluster brand name: Phonetically, "cinna" is almost identical in sound to the word "sinner." Surely the folks at Post noticed this negative. Next, it's unclear that "cinna" is shorthand for the spice "cinnamon." So the obvious question arises: What's a Sinner-Cluster for people who hear the name for the first time? Yes, there are words in the English language that you can truncate like "Fed" for Federal or "Cosmo" for cosmopolitan and the meaning of the shortened word is understood by most people. Unfortunately, "cinnamon" is not one of those words. Lastly, according to forty women—ages 25 to 50—that my firm polled, Cinna-Cluster is a lousy name for a food product. They ranked Kellogg's Raisin Bran (with sales of $199 million in 1999) No. 1 in best phonetic sound for a cereal brand name. It's simple for people to say, and they know what it is. Sometimes, to hit a brand slam, it makes more sense to go with actual words like Kellogg's Frosted Flakes and General Mills' Total Raisin Bran.

Now, let's imagine that a cereal brand manager at a big food company has been given a $1 million budget to bring to life a new cereal product's brand identity. Here's what I would suggest she do to achieve a WOW presentation to management.

Since the brand's name is king, hire a top naming specialist with a proven track record of success to come up with three great cereal brand names. Then immediately file for a claim of trademark ownership under the "Intent to Use" rules of the U.S. Patent & Trademark Office. Don't flinch at a brand name development cost of $150,000 to $200,000. If Nabisco's Oreo cookie brand name were on the auction block today, it would fetch bids in the billions. Company executives who say, "We'll never spend more than $10,000 for brand name recommendations" are part of the reason why so many companies never hit a brand slam with their new product's brand identity.

Next, I would suggest that she spend $150,000 to $200,000 to develop a logo and package design that captures the essence, uniqueness, and spirit of each of the three finalist brand names.

Then I would recommend that she spend whatever it costs to have several hundred boxes printed up for each of the three finalist brands with the new cereal sealed inside each box—as if it were the actual product that you would find on a supermarket shelf.

---

2. Source: *"Cinna-Cluster Targets Adult Cereal Consumers"* by Stephanie Thompson (*Advertising Age, April 10, 2000*).

Next, she should have a production company install a sixty-foot grocery aisle in a convention center, and stock the shelves of the aisle with the boxes of the new cereal featuring the three finalist brand names, logos, and package designs. The grocery aisle also would be stacked with the same number of boxes of competing cereal brands. Yes, we're talking about sixty running feet of packaged brand cereals in all categories. Remember, we're out to achieve WOW.

While all of this is underway, she should have the ad agency assigned to the new cereal brand produce a video of consumers expressing their candid opinions of the finalist brand names, logos, and packaging designs to be shown on a giant screen at the convention center.

Then I would advise her to send out invitations for a cocktail party to several hundred company executives, suppliers, ad and PR agency people, and the press to preview the finalist brands for the new cereal product displayed in the mock-up retail selling environment.

We all know that a brand's name, graphics, package design, and colors will influence our taste sensation to any food or beverage product. So the brand manager should have the invited guests take a taste challenge of the new cereal product packaged in each of the three different boxes and then have them enter their score electronically. That will enable the company's top brass to see on the giant screen what brand name, logo and package design the people at the event have voted first, second, and third.

Finally, I would insist that she spend $150,000 to have 300 consumers preview the cereal boxes stacked on the shelves of the mock-up grocery aisle. These individuals would respond to brand image questions and take the same product taste challenge. With that data in hand, management should be able to make a decision on what brand name and package design to go with.

LESSONS LEARNED

Success depends on how people view the brand you developed. Much of their assessment is influenced by the way your work is presented to them. Take the time, spend the money, and gather the resources to develop and present a brand slam. Vincent Van Gogh sold only one painting in his lifetime. The buyer was his brother, Theodore. Now his paintings are hung on the walls of the world's most famous art museums and sell for $30 million to $60 million at Christie's or Sotheby's auction houses in New York and London.

3

DEFY SAFELY
ENSCONCED TRENDS

*In baseball, your best chance of getting on base is to hit into
an area that's not covered by an opposing fielder. The same is
true when you're in the game to hit a brand slam.*

Companies that hit brand slams do so by defying safely ensconced
product or business trends. They are the masters of the marketing
universe regardless of their industry, size, or geographical reach.
They don't follow in other companies' footsteps, and they break their own
product milestones. These companies aren't interested in creating what the
media and others call new business trends. For them, mastering uncharted
seas is what it's all about.

*A breakthrough product, a new way of doing things, or a revival of an old
classic—this is how business trends begin. Ironically, when a new trend evolves into
a standardized format that most companies conform to, it inevitably leads to the
death of product innovation and creativity.* Apple is credited for having developed mouse technology, which is now standard equipment on every PC
manufactured. How long will it be before this point-and-click device is replaced with a superior product? With the rapid pace of technology, many
industry gurus predict that the mouse will be obsolete by 2003. Don't you
think that an innovative company like Apple is trying to develop that new
technology?

Every CEO in America should pass along the above statement to his or
her company's board of directors. A conformity to trends is a sure sign that
your company is not breaking new ground.

FINALLY, THERE'S JUSTICE IN TELECOMMUNICATIONS

When you and your competitors fall victim to complying with industry trends, a long-term battle of trench warfare is inevitable—that is, until an enterprising company comes along with a better mousetrap or a new way of doing things. Then your company will find itself struggling to keep up with your industry's brightest new star and to escape from the trenches it dug for itself.

One such bright star in the emerging telecommunications business is Culver City, California-based Justice Technology Corporation, which took the top-spot of the 1998 *Inc.* 500—*Inc.* magazine's annual list of America's fastest-growing companies.

With an astonishing five-year growth rate of 27,000 percent (that's right, 27,000 percent!), almost everything about Justice defies the safely ensconced trends prevalent in its industry. The company, with $55.3 million in revenues for 1997, started out selling "callback" services to businesses in Argentina, Brazil, and other South American countries where local phone companies charge exorbitant fees for international calls. Justice's services allow foreign customers to make international calls at cheaper U.S. rates instead of the expensive international rates.

According to *Inc.*, Justice's meteoric growth was owed largely to its founder David Glickman and his relentless drive to expand into new ventures, often without knowing whether or not he was capable of delivering the product to the customer. "I didn't feel comfortable unless I was bringing us out on a limb of a limb of a limb," Glickman told *Inc.* "We'd have to turn the company upside down to make it happen, but that's when things get fun. It's what we all thrive on here."

Unlike its regimented long-distance competitors, the 127 employees at Justice enjoy free lunches, can bring their pets to work, and can use pool tables for daytime fun breaks. Needless to say, casual dress is the norm at Justice. But what speaks volumes about this company's defiance of its competitors' pricing policies is echoed loud and clear in its name—Justice.

History has shown that breaking from safely ensconced business trends can enable a company to lure customers away from its competitors. You will not only stand out from the herd, but also lead the herd.

THE PROBLEM WITH AUTOMATED PHONE SYSTEMS

One way to break from trends is to find an annoying one and distance yourself from it. Take automated telephone operators. Remember those good-old days before automated voice-recorded menu selection? A time when you could place a call to any business in the United States and actually hear a human being's voice on the other end of the line? A time when a knowledgeable operator could answer your inquiry in a matter of fifteen seconds or less, or transfer your call to a person within the company's ranks to address your needs in just seconds? Today, it's rare to contact any company by telephone without hearing that dreaded automated voice-recorded menu. In fact, the entire automated phone system seems to be deliberately crafted to get you lost, frustrated, or on the verge of having a panic attack.

Call your local or regional utility company and see how long it takes to surf the voice-recorded menus before you actually get to speak to a human being. Call a city, state, or federal government agency and be prepared to spend an hour listening to automated voice-recorded messages before you make human contact.

It doesn't take a rocket scientist to figure out that if your company defied this obvious trend by having all incoming calls answered by trained representatives, you would have a tremendous business edge over your competitors. You would also have a big idea for a nationwide TV and print advertising campaign. I can envision the ad's headline now: "We have real people to take your calls, not voice-recorded menus."

HOW AT&T LOST A CUSTOMER'S BUSINESS

Now you would think that if anyone knew how to perfect a voice-activated communications system, it would be a company that has been in the telecommunications business for 100-plus years. My friend Sandy relates this story:

> In early 2000, it came to my attention that AT&T hadn't billed my company for three months for long-distance calls. It turned out that AT&T was sending our monthly billing statements to another firm in San Francisco that had no relationship to our firm. Without a phone call, email, fax, or letter notice, our long-distance service was cut off for nonpayment of bills. Well, how can you pay a bill if you don't get one? I was so ticked off that I personally called AT&T's customer service department.
>
> The voice-activated instruction began: "Please enter your 13-digit account number now." No sooner had I entered the first three account numbers, 020, when I heard, "Sorry, but I do not recognize the number 597, please reenter your account number." Again, after hitting the numbers 020 on my phone's touch pad, I heard, "Sorry, but I don't recognize the number 783, please . . ."
>
> I shouted back into the handset, "I entered 020, not 783." Realizing I had a long row to hoe, I decided to go to

menu option number two—pay bill by credit card. I thought that if I paid the outstanding bill we never received electronically, possibly our long-distance service would be restored within hours. The voice instruction asked me "To pay your bill by credit card, please say Visa or MasterCard now."

"MasterCard," I said loud and clear.

"Please say Visa or MasterCard, now!" was what I heard again, and I said the latter again.

On what seemed like the tenth try, I yelled out, "It's MasterCard, you idiots."

"We cannot assist you any further, thank you for calling AT&T customer service." I was disconnected. I called back only to hear the menu options repeated again.

I called it a day with AT&T.

This story is typical not only with AT&T—whose customer service is notoriously bad—but also with other major companies. I suggest to the top executives running AT&T that they try dealing with the automated service, to see what it's like to be a small business customer for one day dealing with AT&T by phone. The morning could be spent trying to resolve a simple billing problem with AT&T's business customer service. Nothing beats being in the customer's shoes to see things from a new perspective. I'm sure you have your own horror stories about voice-recorded menus.

The point is, when you can offer consumers a better way of doing business than that of your competitors, you've got the making of a WOW ad campaign. Then it's just a matter of telling your story in a compelling way in TV commercials and through other advertising vehicles.

HERTZ KEEPS ITS CUSTOMERS DRY

One company that has created WOW with its advertising is Hertz. I'm sure you have seen the commercials boasting that when you choose Hertz you'll find covered canopies for its rental cars at all major airports in the event of an unexpected downpour. The same TV spots show two businessmen soaking wet in a competing car-rental location. Now that's what I call a brand slam ad.

In most cases, defying trends is simply a matter of looking at the products in your industry that have become accepted by consumers but can be vastly improved with engineering or design.

FEWER WIRES, BRIGHTER COLORS PAY OFF FOR APPLE

Chances are you use a PC at home. If you're like me and millions of other people around the world who rely on such computers for word processing, Web access, or online banking, you know what it's like to deal with the entanglement of wires. There are wires that hook up your computer tower to your monitor, wires for the media console, keyboard, speakers, printer, and power surge unit. Simply put, there's probably an unsightly mess of wires dangling off your work desk and onto the floor.

Apple, under Steve Jobs' leadership, had the vision to change the desktop computer by eliminating this maze of wiring. The product: iMac. Not only does it get high marks in product design, you only need to plug in two cords to run the iMac with Internet access. It's also the first PC ever to be offered in a variety of bright colors to match any room's decor. Now that's what I call a big idea that defies an industry trend and benefits Apple's employees, shareholders, and customers.

To defy trends takes imagination, commitment to a new way of doing things, and an attitude-driven mentality on the part of management to do what it takes to succeed. There are possibilities to defy business trends in every industry. By taking risks, management can pave the way for greater revenues and profits. Taking risks is especially important for those old-economy companies with slow growth potential. Let's look at the possibilities.

REWARD LONGTIME CUSTOMERS

Most companies are not known for rewarding customers who have a long-time relationship with them. Want to hit a brand slam this year? It's simple. Just come up with a breakaway product that's based on the length of time customers have been loyal to your brand.

Marketers need to do more than give lip service in their ads to relationship marketing or they run the risk of losing valued customers to competitors who do a better job at creating relationships. Let me relate the story of my friend David.

David has been an American Express Gold Card member since 1972. The annual fees he's paid over that time have totaled about $2,100. But that's taxi fare when you take into account the merchants' fees American Express received on all of the purchases David charged to his Gold Card for almost three decades. That number is probably a whopping $50,000. He also paid about $3,000 in interest fees on his American Express Optimum account over those years at rates hovering around 20 percent annually. Yet, after demonstrating almost thirty years of loyalty to this brand, the Gold Card people at American Express never once offered David something special that it wouldn't give to anyone else who signs up today for a

Gold Card and has yet to generate a dollar of revenue or profit for the company. Is this the product of corporate greed, or is it not knowing how to build customer relationships that go on for decades? Maybe a little of both!

In early 2000, David got an offer from MasterCard that was too good to pass up. No annual card fee and a 10 percent fixed interest rate should he wish to carry a balance—half the amount of what American Express charges if you activate your American Express Optima account, which is linked to your Gold Card. David asked the Gold Card people if they would waive the annual card fee of $75 and match MasterCard's fixed interest rate. The answer was no. What do you think David did?

DEFY STANDARDIZED ARCHITECTURAL DESIGNS

The "big three" burger chains—McDonald's, Burger King, and Wendy's—sometimes think that they are bucking trends by adding a melted hot pepper cheddar cheese sauce on the beef's patty or throwing in a few fried onion rings with the purchase of a burger. Let's get real. This isn't defying trends—it's simply a new spin on burger toppings. Now here's a way for one of the big three and others in the fast-food industry to defy a standardized trend.

The architectural design of freestanding fast-food burger, pizza, and Mexican restaurants are essentially a shoe box with a distinctive roof design. The facility is placed on a plot of land paved with asphalt for customer parking. When you enter one of these eateries, the selling environment is predictable. You walk past rows of laminated wood tables and plastic-molded chairs until you reach a counter where you place your order. After fifty years of fast-food eateries in America, you would think that one of the major players would shake up the industry with an innovative restaurant design and food-service experience.

Of course, the management of these chains will tell you that it can't be done, it's not economically feasible. "It can't be done" is what some of the best minds in computer programming told Steve Jobs when he set out to replace Apple's PC DOS system with a new system based on menus and icons.

Go to a main U.S. postal service center in any major city in America, a flagship bank in any state in this country, a big city airport, a state motor vehicle center, a city or federal government building and what do they have in common? Answer: Vast open spaces and what looks like miles of granite flooring. Employees who serve the public are stationed behind windowed stalls or counters located at the farthest point from the building's main entrance. Is anyone thinking about revamping these wide open spaces to create a new and better experience?

I don't buy the idea that all of the vast open spaces are needed for traffic flow. Everyday, thousands of consumers flow through the main floor of Bloomingdale's flagship store on Third Avenue and Sixtieth Street in midtown Manhattan. They have little problem negotiating around one hundred or more brand-name boutiques that fill this one square block of retail space. In fact, these glamorous boutiques offer perhaps the largest collection of internationally renowned perfumes, cosmetics, designer watches, sunglasses, and other personal goods in one convenient location. Bloomingdale's main floor is a "must see" experience for thousands of tourists visiting the Big Apple each week.

NEW YORK CITY'S AMAZING TURNAROUND

Here's another example of how a city made a revolutionary change. For ten years, I commuted by train from Bronxville, New York, to my firm's midtown office in Manhattan. That meant walking through Grand Central Terminal twice a day. Except for the famous Oyster Bar & Restaurant on the lower level, Zaro's Bread Basket shop on the main level, magazine and newspaper stands, and an open bar terrace located near the terminal's Vanderbilt Street entrance on the west side, there was little reason to explore one of America's great landmark buildings. If you entered the terminal from 42nd Street or Lexington Avenue, you were greeted by unfortunate souls sleeping in the walkways or on benches. But times have changed since the late 1980s and early 1990s.

After a four-year monumental effort, Grand Central Terminal has been revitalized, and it's even greater than it was when it first opened in 1913. It's a brand slam for the 500,000 commuters who walk through the terminal's world famous Main Concourse each day. It's on the top ten list of "must places" to tour if you're visiting New York. Today, the terminal is unlike any other attraction in the heart of midtown. It's home to about forty retail stores, seventeen restaurants, and a spectacular food market where you can buy—from fourteen different merchants—German hams and sausages, cheeses from around the world, fresh meat, poultry and fish, produce fruit, wild edibles, spices, herbs, breads, and pastries. A good friend of mine, Al Drefs, who lives on Manhattan's West Side takes a cross-town bus to Grand Central Terminal to buy groceries for the week. Now when a New Yorker is willing to deal with cross-town traffic during the lunch hour, there must be a good reason. Or, something wonderful is awaiting him at his destination.

The revitalized terminal attracts celebrities from around the world to give live performances in the Main Concourse. Carly Simon's free concert performance made front-page news and was picked up by all of the TV news networks. Art exhibits like the award-winning ad campaigns of

Absolut Vodka draw thousands of people to the terminal. What was once a mammoth dreary-looking building comprised of seven acres of prime Manhattan land, has been transformed into a celestial showplace. In a way, it sort of reflects the celestial stars and astrological signs that adorn the terminal's domed ceiling.

THINK OUTSIDE THE BOX

When you see a Volkswagen New Beetle parked on a street, the manufacturer's name instantly comes to mind. No other car even resembles it. By reintroducing its classic Beetle in early 1998, featuring an aerodynamic look and an eye-popping ergonomic interior design, Volkswagen has defied the automotive trends of the 1990s.

The Ford Taurus and its sister Mercury Sable are built on the same platform and feature the same powertrain. Except for minor exterior and interior trim differences, they are essentially the same vehicle. The Ford Contour and its sister Mercury Mystique are even more identical. Here's the kicker: These four car lines built by Ford are advertised to consumers as being uniquely different vehicles. But for every six Ford Taurus and Contour cars sold in America, only one Sable or Mystique car is sold. Here's my advice to Ford: Build and design Mercury-branded cars (like the Mercury Cougar) that stand apart from all competitive cars including Ford-branded products. If Ford Motor pulled that off, the unit sales of Mercury-branded cars might just rival Ford-branded cars. It doesn't make sense to have Ford and Mercury cars that are identical. Create a new identity for Mercury. For the almost 1,000 independent Mercury dealerships in America, that idea holds the promise of a brand slam.

The Cadillac Motor Car Company, GM's flagship car division, has an impressive history of defying automotive trends. Cadillac's long list of automotive innovations dates back to the early twentieth century. Its Northstar system remains unmatched in the automotive industry today. Cadillac Sevilles, DeVilles, and Eldorados all use this precise orchestration of powertrain and chassis technology to deliver superior power, control, reliability, safety, and efficiency. Cadillac's OnStar system has been so successful that all GM-made cars will eventually have this onboard satellite-link communications system. And Cadillac was the first to introduce Night Vision in a car.

But aside from all of the accolades that Cadillac has received from the auto trade and the nation's press for setting a higher standard in automotive engineering, it made serious blunders in brand management throughout the 1980s. Management allowed this world-class brand to fall into the trap of conformity. To save money on manufacturing tooling, GM stamped out Cadillac-branded cars that were look-a-likes to Oldsmobile and Buick cars. It didn't take long for Cadillac's main rival, Ford's Lincoln division, to remind affluent consumers in TV commercials that when you buy a Cadillac you're really getting an Oldsmobile. Then Cadillac introduced an entry-level four-door sedan called Cimarron that was not even worthy of the Chevrolet badge, let alone the legendary Cadillac wreath and crest symbol. If that wasn't bad enough, Cadillac lost face when it discontinued production of its much-touted Allante 2-door roadster because of disappointing sales.

Keep in mind that from the 1930s through the mid-1970s, the Cadillac brand was considered by business and government leaders world over to be the "gold standard of excellence" by which all products and companies were measured. Cadillac lost that title to other premium brands like Mercedes-Benz and Lexus. Can this legendary brand ever regain the most cherished title to be held by any manufacturer in the world? If it keeps hitting brand slams with the fusion of product design and technology as exemplified in the stunning new DeVille DHS, there's a good chance it will. The Cadillac DeVille was America's No. 1 best-selling luxury car in 1999.

In a Cadillac TV commercial aired in 1999, we see people walking along Main Street U.S.A. turning their heads to catch a glimpse of a stunning blonde behind the wheel of a vintage red Cadillac convertible with those tailfins that have been immortalized in American history along with images of Marilyn Monroe and Elvis Presley. Then we see a guy in his fifties behind the wheel of a 2000 Cadillac sedan. As both cars pass each other, an actor's voiceover reminds us that a Cadillac never fails to get our attention. But in truth, the 2000 Cadillac is no match compared to that classic tailfin wonder. My advice to Cadillac: Bring back those nostalgic tailfins in a new aerodynamic car design and, like the New Beetle, watch the car's sales soar off the charts.

In fact, one car company embraced a unique retro design and sales have skyrocketed since. Have you seen Chrysler's PT Cruiser? It's officially classified as a truck but in actuality, it's a new vehicle segment. It combines elements of a minivan, a sport utility vehicle or SUV, a London black cab, and most of all, a '38 Chevy Tudor sedan. "It is the most striking looking ride on the road," stated Bob Garfield, *Advertising Age* critic, about the new Chrysler PT Cruiser.[1] According to Garfield, the PT Cruiser targets young singles and married couples who currently own small cars that couldn't transport a washing machine, such as the Honda Civic.

Like the New Beetle, nothing comes even close to matching the PT Cruiser in automotive design. It's a retro-1940s hot rod with a high-racked roof line and bulging fenders over the front wheels. If the exterior is the bait, then the interior is the hook. There are 26 combinations of how you can arrange the seating and back shelf in the huge interior. In short, it's an

---

1. *"Chrysler Hits Right Buttons to Unveil PT Cruiser"* by Bob Garfield (Advertising Age, April 17, 2000).

excellent example of a breakaway vehicle that sells at an affordable price—between $16,000 and $19,000. Garfield added, "Chrysler won't be able to manufacture enough of them to meet demand.[2]

As of August 1, 2000, Chrysler's PT Cruiser sells off dealer lots in eight days on average. This compares to other Chrysler vehicles that take an average of fifty-five days for dealers to sell. Waiting time to get a PT Cruiser is up to eight months at some dealerships. By the way, "PT" stands for "personal transportation." I thought it was a play on the U.S. Navy's "PT Boats" dating back to World War II.

A WAKE-UP CALL TO CEOs

Everything I've said so far is meant to send a wake-up call to CEOs about the dangers of becoming trend worshippers. If you're not developing breakaway products and redefining the product category itself, finding better ways of doing business with your customers, and providing the best return on investment, your company may not be around for very long. It's irrelevant if your accomplishments get labeled as new trends. The message here is simple and clear: Defy trends for more revenues, more profits, and increased market share.

In late March 1999, Fidelity Investments, which stars Peter Lynch, the company's former market fund guru in its TV spots, sent a letter to its 30,000 customers. The letter informed customers that they're making too many calls to the company's representatives to inquire about how their funds are doing. Fidelity noted that it's too costly to provide this personalized service on a day-to-day basis.

This is tantamount to McDonald's announcing in a global TV spot that it's costing too much money to prepare and package menu items. From now on, when you and your kids visit a McDonald's restaurant, be prepared to cook and package your own food and dispense your own beverages. Of course, menu prices wouldn't change. Wouldn't Burger King and Wendy's love to hear that news?

Corporate number crunchers are great at looking for ways to save a company a dime here or there. But most accountants have blinders on when it comes to understanding how you build a standout customer service experience that results in a brand slam. Personalized customer service happens to be one of the hallmarks that built Fidelity into a mutual fund powerhouse.

When customer service—built on years of tradition—is diminished to save on operational expenses, savvy marketing leaders find a way to turn

---

2. *Ibid.*

the picture around so that it comes out looking like it's a benefit to the customer. Therein lies the genius of brand management. One option Fidelity had was to provide its customers with personalized online account information.

LESSONS LEARNED

1. When enough people tell you it can't be done, you know you're moving in the right direction to achieve WOW.

2. A pattern of marketing "faux pas" in one form or another will always occur among industry giants. When the leaders don't see it but you do, there's your golden opportunity to hit a brand slam and take away the market share.

3. Defying trends is simply a matter of looking at the products in your industry that have become accepted by consumers but can be vastly improved in engineering, design, or communication.

4. Hand over product design decisions to the number crunchers and the "love" for the product will go right out the window.

5. Don't talk about relationship marketing with valued customers— do it.

4

OLDIES BUT GOODIES

"Thanks for the memories."
                            Bob Hope's musical introduction

I mentioned in my book *The Omnipowerful Brand* that many retired brand icons were due for a comeback. Why? Because there's nothing more powerful in a company's brand arsenal than a brand icon that consumers have come to know, admire, and trust. Here are a few of the old classics that have returned in a big way.

THE WORLD'S MOST RECOGNIZED GLASS BOTTLE

In mid-March 2000, Coca-Cola announced it was bringing back "the original" Coke glass bottle with the pry-off metal cap. Few marketers have as many powerhouse brand icons as the world's No. 1 soft drink maker. Its impressive list includes Coca-Cola Classic, Coke, and Diet Coke brand names and logos; the Coca-Cola deep red color; the Coca-Cola graphic bottle cap; and the brand's white swirl design inspired by the original Coke glass bottle. Then there are the Coca-Cola stores and the computer-animated family of polar bears in the TV ad spots who get a laugh from us when they playfully belch after downing a big bottle of "The Real Thing." So, with all these brand images, why bring back the original Coke glass bottle?

Coca-Cola needs to assure Wall Street, investors, employees, suppliers, and consumers that it hasn't lost its brand marketing prowess. There's been uncertainty created by management change at the top, lower than expected earnings performance, the layoff of 5,000 white collar workers at the company's Atlanta-based headquarters, and a recall of products in

Europe due to bottle contamination. In short, Coca-Cola needed some piz-zazz and positive press. It got just that and more with the announcement of the return of the original Coke bottle. Remember, Coca-Cola's selling image is lifestyle first, the actual dark-brew carbonated soft drinks come second.

Coca-Cola's image is intact, but it needs to hit brand slams to stay on top. It can't just get a runner on first, or even on second. It has to continue bringing the crowd to its feet—that's what has made the Coca-Cola brand an enduring icon.

PEPSI IS BACK WITH THE CHALLENGE

Your next-door neighbor buys a new Buick Park Avenue and now you're out shopping for a new Cadillac DeVille DHS with OnStar satellite-link communication and Night Vision. Since I can remember, Pepsi seems to be in the business of trying to get Coca-Cola to blink. A week after Coca-Cola announced the return of the original Coke bottle, Pepsi announced that it was bringing back the "Pepsi Challenge" TV ad campaign, which stopped airing in 1977.

The Pepsi Challenge was a big idea in advertising campaigns of the past half century. People appearing in the TV spots said they preferred the taste refreshment of Pepsi over Coke after accepting the challenge to taste both colas in a blind test. Of course, only people preferring Pepsi over Coke ap-peared in the spots. So effective were these commercials, that Pepsi got Coca-Cola's management to blink, and blink again, every time Pepsi won the taste challenge.

To mount a counterattack, Coca-Cola spent millions of dollars experi-menting with and testing new Coke recipes with consumers in all of its markets. The research findings convinced Coca-Cola's then top brass that its soft drink brew masters had come up with a better tasting Coke. So "New Coke"—a slightly sweeter version of the original Coke recipe—was launched in an all-out around-the-clock advertising and public relations blitz. It was a high-stakes gamble, tampering with a product that had been advertised and promoted globally for generations as "Original Coke" and "The Real Thing."

There was such a national outcry of "How could you do this to us?" by Coke enthusiasts that management reversed itself and took New Coke off the market and brought back the original Coke product under the new brand name "Coca-Cola Classic." Ironically, what many in the advertising business called the biggest fiasco in the management of a brand icon turned out to be a brand slam for Coca-Cola Classic.

Unless you're over thirty, there's no way you could remember those great Pepsi Challenge commercials. That means Pepsi's advertising agency is starting from scratch to build awareness of the Pepsi Challenge with the target buyer audience for Pepsi consumption. In contrast, the same youthful audience for Coke consumption pretty much knows what the original Coke bottle looks like from variations on the bottle's design and the bottle's appearance in Coca-Cola commercials.

The jury is still out as to whether the return of the Pepsi Challenge commercial will make the king of colas blink again. Even if it doesn't, I predict that millions of teens around the world will take the Pepsi Challenge. That in itself would score a brand slam advertising hit for Pepsi.

"CHARLIE THE TUNA" RETURNS

On May 24, 1999, America's favorite spokesfish, "Charlie the Tuna," returned to the television screen to tout StarKist's new, improved solid white albacore. In his first appearance in a new ad campaign in almost 10 years, Charlie was a big hit with a new generation of tuna sandwich aficionados— boys and girls who hadn't seen his other 85 commercials simply because they weren't born yet. A slightly slimmer, more modern Charlie in a luminous blue skin looks fresher than ever thanks to computer-generated animation that wasn't around in 1961 when Charlie made his first commercial guest appearance for StarKist Seafood, an affiliate of the H.J. Heinz Company. "There is no better way to capture attention and build loyalty for this new StarKist product than by using our strongest, most beloved spokesperson, Charlie," said Joe Clancy, group vice president of sales and marketing.

HERE COMES "ELSIE THE COW"

The Dairy Farmers of America decided to bring back "Elsie the Cow" on product packaging and labeling. Named as one of the top ten brand icons of all time by *Advertising Age,* this barnyard queen, always adorned with fresh daisies around her neck, has come to symbolize the Borden brand's heritage of wholesome and affordable dairy products. While there's only one living Jerry Seinfeld pitch man for the American Express Card, there have been some fifty "live" Borden Elsies since 1939.

Here's some trivia about Elsie that you may not know. This brand icon served her country well—in the early 1940s, Elsie raised $10 million in War Bonds by going on national tour. She made her first Hollywood film debut as a cow named "Buttercup" in the movie *Little Man,* starring Jack Oakie and Kay Francis. Elsie has been presented with keys to over 200 cities. She celebrated her sixtieth commercial birthday on October 26, 1999. DFA, a farming cooperative founded in early 1998 (an outgrowth formed by four regional dairy-producer cooperatives), held the barnyard bash that reintroduced Elsie in New York City's Bryant Park.

WELCOME BACK, MR. WHIPPLE

The return of Mr. Whipple in June 1999, was among the most memorable advertising brand slams to close out the twentieth century. But then, Charmin has a history of hitting brand slams. Maybe that's why people prefer Charmin over the other leading competitor, Northern, by almost 3-to-1 according to *Advertising Age*.

After a fourteen-year hiatus, actor Dick Wilson, also known as "Mr. Whipple" to millions of homemakers, returned to star in new TV spots for Procter & Gamble's upgraded Charmin branded bath tissue. Even with a few deeper lines on his forehead, Mr. Whipple's face is as well-known to Americans as the faces of Michael Jordan, Billy Graham, and Bill Clinton. Mr. Whipple, who earned TV fame by saying, "Please don't squeeze the Charmin!" is back to tell us that Charmin is now soft as pillows and even stronger than ever.

America's favorite bath tissue brand began in 1928, when Charmin was manufactured by Hoberg Paper Company in Green Bay, Wisconsin. The inspiration for the brand's name came from an employee who described the soft, strong, and absorbent tissue as being "charming." That adjective led to the word *Charmin* (pronounced "shar - min"). When P&G acquired the company in 1957, management knew it had the potential of a brand slam with the Charmin brand and the then-theme slogan "Charmin Babies Your Skin" on the product's packaging.

While it's commonplace today to find a 12-roll package of bath tissue paper in supermarkets and drugstores, the introduction of a Charmin 4-roll package in 1932, was a brand slam for parents with teenagers. Back then, this was innovative product packaging.

Charmin hit three brand slams in 1964. The first came with the creation of the Mr. Whipple character to promote Charmin's "squeezable softness." The character was so believable and liked by homemakers, that Mr. Whipple appeared for more than 20 years in Charmin television, radio, and print ads. The second brand slam came with the creation of what many marketing people call the most recognizable slogan in the annals of advertising history. "Please don't squeeze the Charmin!" did just what it was intended to do: Get millions of curious homemakers to squeeze a Charmin roll. By doing so, they discovered for themselves how much softer Charmin was to other leading bath tissue brands, including private labels. The third brand slam came when Charmin was the first to add a scented fragrance to a bath tissue.

I enjoy relating the history of Charmin to new recruits in brand management. Why? It's a story about toilet paper, and that sounds like a prison sentence for any brand manager. Yet the people who have taken their turn to manage Charmin over the last seventy years have shown us all that building a toilet paper brand can be a true challenge and great fun. Think about it. If you were stranded on an island, what would you rather have in your possession: $1,000 in American Express travelers cheques, or the equivalent amount of money in twelve-roll packages of Charmin?

SPEEDY'S BACK, ALONG WITH "PLOP, PLOP, FIZZ, FIZZ"

Alka-Seltzer's animated "Speedy" character returned in TV commercials in 1997 to tell us that all it takes is "plop, plop, fizz, fizz" for an effervescent antacid and pain relief medicine. The person who came up with the "plop, plop, fizz, fizz" brand slogan is a marketing genius. In just four short words, you know how to dispense the product and when the product is ready to be gulped down. Now if that's not a brand slam ad slogan, then tell me what is. But there's more. Those four memorable words have racked up hundreds of millions of dollars of Alka-Seltzer sales that might never have been realized. How? The words *plop, plop* remind us to drop two tablets (not one tablet) of Alka-Seltzer into a glass of water, thus, doubling the product's per capita consumption since the 1950s. Without the "plop, plop," most people would have dissolved only one tablet in water.

In 1956, Speedy was the first animated character to appear on TV to promote a product. After an incredible fourteen-year run in TV and print advertisements, the child-like Speedy character and the "plop, plop, fizz, fizz" slogan were replaced with live actors and new ad campaigns. Some of these TV spots were hilarious with an actor in great pain saying: "I can't believe I ate the whole thing," or "Mamma mia, that was a spicy meatball." People remembered these humorous lines, but didn't necessarily remember to take Alka-Seltzer when they had an acid attack. I guess the people at Bayer's Consumer Products group realized that on this planet, only one product goes "plop, plop, fizz, fizz" and that's Alka-Seltzer. Hats off to you Bayer for bringing back one of the greatest brand lines ever created in the annals of advertising history.

A NEW PEACOCK RETURNS TO NBC

Most company brand logos or symbols are retired because the new CEO wants his or her thumbprint to appear on the company's trademark. But most retired company brand logos or symbols return to appear in full glory because the new CEO eventually recognizes the genius that went into the original work. NBC's history of playing musical chairs with the network's trademark comes to mind.

The nation's first permanent broadcasting network, NBC has introduced to the public seven different brand logos or symbols in a time span covering less than sixty years. That averages out to be a new brand trademark every eight years. In contrast, ABC and CBS network brand logos have endured for more than four decades. CNN, the most respected and watched cable news network in the world, has not retired the CNN logo that first debuted in 1980.

In 1943, NBC got its first official logo, a microphone surrounded by lightning bolts. The second logo aired on New Year's day, 1954. It was a depiction of a stylized xylophone and mallet, accompanied by the three chimes first heard on NBC radio in 1927. Being the first network to broadcast in "living color," NBC introduced its third logo in 1956. It was dubbed "The Bird"—an eleven-feathered Peacock in six colors that was flashed at the beginning and end of color shows. To the surprise of many at that time, a new leadership team dumped the striking Peacock symbol. The network's new logo was introduced in 1959. It drew the nickname "The Snake" because the letters "NBC" were connected in one continuous line and animated on TV to "grow" from the "N" letter to form a stacked typographic logo. In 1974, a new management team decided it was time to invent a more modern logo and hired my former employer Lippincott & Margulies to come up with the design. Just prior to the development of NBC's logo designs, I left L&M to form my own brand identity firm.

The late Walter Margulies, chairman and cofounder of the firm still bearing his name, persuaded NBC's then president to identify the broadcasting network simply with the "N" letter. The logic being that TV viewers would know that "N" stood for NBC. Obviously, someone failed to point out that "NBC" is already a truncated name for National Broadcasting Company. So NBC ended up being the first industry giant in America to my knowledge to have selected a truncation of a truncated name for its brand identity. Fortunately, other giants didn't follow NBC. Otherwise we would have "I" for IBM, "G" for GM, and "P" for P&G.

The accepted "N" symbol was a geometrical design consisting of two trapezoids—one red, one blue. Shortly after the new symbol aired nationwide on New Year's Day 1975, NBC's management got the news that the "N" design and color scheme were identical to the logo of a small Nebraska TV station. The news made front-page headlines. The question of plagiarism was never resolved because NBC settled with the other station for a sum of $750,000, as reported in *The New York Times*. Thus, the abstract "N" survived, but not for long. In 1980, a new management team introduced "The Proud N." The design featured a new Peacock with eleven feathers appearing in the center of the "N" design.

In 1986, NBC finally hit a brand slam with its new brand identity. Again, under new management leadership, "The Bird" returned to its place as NBC's proud symbol. With its six feathers representing the network's six divisions, this peacock remains one of the world's most recognized symbols. Simplicity, clarity, and timelessness are the hallmarks of this exceptional trademark that stands above any broadcasting or cable network's logo or symbol. That adds up to WOW in my book.

LESSONS LEARNED

1. If it's not broken, don't fix it.
2. People instinctively love mascots. Look what Mickey Mouse did for Disney and Bugs Bunny did for Warner Bros.

5

IT TAKES VISION, COURAGE, DETERMINATION, TALENT, AND MORE

Archival black-and-white film footage shows George Herman "Babe" Ruth in the batter's box in a 1932 World Series game at Wrigley Field between the New York Yankees and the Chicago Cubs. Booed by Cubs fans and with two strikes facing him, Ruth raises his arm, and points two fingers in the direction of the park's center field fence. The Babe called the spot where his home run would fly. The pitch is delivered and the rest is forever immortalized in baseball history. It takes the same vision, courage, determination, and talent to hit a brand slam in business.

VISION

True, some brand slams in the twentieth century happened by chance or good timing. But if you're out to hit a brand slam today, it takes extraordinary vision to pull it off. It's a matter of knowing where you're going and staying focused until you get there.

What makes one CEO possess the vision to give the green light to develop and launch new brands, while another CEO merely acts as a caretaker of established brand assets? To answer this question would require another full-length business book. Yet, I believe I can point you in the right direction with far fewer words. Let's begin by turning to *Webster's* for a meaning of the word *vision:*

> a) The ability to perceive something not actually visible, as through mental acuteness or keen foresight (a project made possible by one man's vision.) b) force or power of imagination . . .

I can't find fault with *Webster's* definition. Yet, in the world of brand slams, I believe my definition has more relevance to achieving WOW.

> Vision—one's ability to look at a blank canvas and imagine the painting that's yet to be painted, knowing full well that as the painting progresses it will change and take on different characteristics from the original thought.

Pablo Picasso, Henri Matisse, Paul Klee, Frank Stella, and other masters of twentieth century art, all had the power of vision that I've just defined. In the business world of the past century, Henry Ford, Alfred P. Sloan Jr., Thomas J. Watson, Jr., Sam Walton, Steven Spielberg, William H. Gates III, Donald Trump, and others, have demonstrated this power of vision, too. Therein lies their genius.

Take Henry Ford (1863–1947). The automobile was invented years before he founded the Ford Motor Company in 1903. Yet Henry Ford's vision was to mass produce America's best built and affordable cars. He hit a brand slam with the public in 1908 when the Ford Model T rolled off the assembly line. In doing so, he went on to build the largest industrial organization of its kind in America and amassed a personal wealth of $1 billion, which was unheard of even to Wall Street tycoons in the early twentieth century. The Model T held the world's car production record until it was broken by the Volkswagen Beetle in 1972. Almost a century later, Henry Ford's vision to build the best affordable cars in America remains the cornerstone of this legendary brand known worldwide simply as Ford.

CEOs that possess the power of vision have entrepreneurial blood running through their veins. They tend to be a different breed from buttoned-down professional managers schooled in the practices of business management at Harvard, Yale, and Princeton. Most also have an itch to break out of their industry's inborn cocoon. Perhaps a downside of their genius is that they seldom receive kudos for their management skills. Yet without entrepreneurs like Apple's Steve Jobs, corporate management is always several steps short of hitting a brand slam. Apple's board of directors learned this lesson the hard way.

Apple's directors ousted Jobs, the company's cofounder, and handed the reins of power over to John Scully. Scully, who held the position of chief marketing officer at PepsiCo, had been hand picked by Jobs to run Apple. The purpose was to free Jobs from day-to-day operational responsibilities. Many Wall Street analysts hailed the change of guard and called

Scully the right person to take Apple to a new level in global brand marketing. But it wasn't long thereafter that Scully departed from Apple. In an industry where the day you launch a new computer product it's surpassed in technology or design the next week by a competitor, Apple's board of directors finally got the message that it needed a CEO with product vision, not a caretaker of existing brand-name product lines. Ironically, some ten years later, with Apple facing its very demise, the board persuaded Jobs to return as chairman and acting CEO.

Having vision for a new product, service experience, or business venture that is yet to be produced or marketed in a tangible form goes beyond merely having an idea for the same. True, everything starts with an idea. But an idea will quickly evaporate without a great visionary to bring that idea to life and to sell it to corporate management or investment bankers. Many great screenplays are turned down because of the studio executive's inability to visualize the end product. Steven Spielberg's genius lies in his ability as a film director to read a script or novel and to see the making of a great motion picture. Thanks to Spielberg's power of vision, people living in future centuries will gain insight on our values in the late twentieth century by viewing such films as *E.T., Schindler's List,* and *Saving Private Ryan.*

When the Internet became more commercialized in 1991, we realized that the power of vision is all it takes for an entrepreneur to become an overnight multimillionaire, or even a billionaire. AOL jumped into the fray to design a program that was easy for people to work with. In the early 1990s, few believed that the Internet could become user-friendly or that it would catch on as a new information medium. AOL's founder Steve Case was advised to put his time and money into something else. Undeterred, Case continued to pursue his vision of building a user-friendly online communications company. Today, AOL is a communications giant. With 24 million members online in the U.S. alone, it is one of the most recognized online brands.

In addition to AOL, Internet companies like Yahoo!, Excite@home, AltaVista, Amazon.com, Double Click, and eBay also have become household brands in just three or four years. Among the newest start-ups, one caught my attention for imagination: AsSeenIn.com. How many times have you watched a TV show and said to yourself: "Gee, I like that sofa, or coffee table, or carpet in the studio set design." Well, thanks to the folks at AsSeenIn.com and with the latest Internet technology, you can visit actual sets from your favorite TV shows and click on the item and learn how to buy it directly from the retailer.

Lessons Learned

1. You can have the courage, determination, and talent to go for a brand slam, but without vision, you'll always be a step short of achieving WOW.

2. Without vision the pipelines that new products, services, and business ventures flow through will shut down.

3. The power of vision takes only one gifted person, not a committee of twenty-five people with different backgrounds. Form a large committee to define the vision of a new product or business venture and the end result will more than likely be a compromise that suits the different agendas of these people.

COURAGE

Going for a brand slam takes guts. Often, management bets a good part of the corporate ranch to hit one. And having announced its intentions to launch a major new product or business venture, it's often putting its company's reputation on the line with Wall Street, investors, employees, suppliers, and consumers.

Looking back over the last century, the Ford Motor Company takes the honors for having the courage to go for a winning brand slam when it was needed the most. Twice it gambled its reputation and the corporate ranch on the success of two automotive lines. First, Henry Ford's Model T launched in 1908, and then the Taurus launched in 1986. Both are incredible stories of design, engineering, manufacturing, and marketing and sales accomplishments. Since I've already discussed the success of the Model T, let's talk about the now-famous Taurus.

In the fall of 1982, my firm was retained by Ford's North American management to develop brand positioning and name recommendations for a revolutionary new breed of Ford sedans and wagons. Ford's car sales in America had plummeted to an all-time low. Its market share fell from 23.6 percent in 1975 to 16.6 percent in 1981. To put it bluntly, Ford needed to hit one hell of a brand slam to regain its automotive footing. The once desirable Ford LTD and sister Mercury Marquis cars had lost their appeal with target buyers of affordable family sedans. Their boxy-looking sheet metal bodies, picnic-like interior bench seats, and nondescript dash boards were no match for the new "Euro-styled" cars offered by BMW, Honda, and Toyota.

Ford's management gave its design and engineering chiefs unlimited Visa card spending to come up with a new flagship car line that would blow away the import competition. In short, Ford mounted an all-out counterattack against the imports to regain market share in the upper-middle car segment.

I met with Ken Smith, Ford's then strategic marketing chief for North American Operations. "Let me be candid," he said. "If Ford is not successful with these new cars, Ford will no longer be in the automotive business." Then he showed me color photos of the new planned breed of Ford aerodynamic sedans and wagons.

The moment my eyes caught sight of these new cars, I responded with one word: WOW! Some carmakers improve a car by 5 percent and they run TV spots inviting the public to "Come see the all-new designed so and so . . ." Not these models. There was nothing that these new cars had in common with the Ford LTD model line of that day.

> "There are two camps within Ford," said Smith. "One is determined to see the LTD badge carried forward on these new Ford cars because the name is well fixed in the minds of consumers. The second wants a European-inspired name—such as Autobahn—to signal to consumers that Ford's new cars will be as good as or better than competitive-priced European rivals. I need your firm to tell us what is the best direction to take. You don't have to give me your answer today."

> "I can tell you now," I replied. "The thinking of both camps is wrong. These new car models are revolutionary in design. The LTD name is like placing and old, tired sofa in a newly decorated living room. These cars deserve a fresh and original name and not a reminder of the past mistakes that Ford has made.

> "A European-inspired name like Autobahn is not believable," I added. "Yes, it could be believable if we were naming a new BMW or Mercedes-Benz car, but it's too great a leap for Ford to make at this point in time. It will sound a false note.

> "Ford cars are American-built, not European-built. The name should sound American and reflect the broad changes in design, engineering, and production that are underway at the Ford Motor Company. These are my thoughts."

> "I agree with your thinking," said Smith. "I want your firm to develop American-sounding names. But I also need a name recommendation that's European-inspired."

> "What about the code name Taurus? Is it legally available?" I asked.

> "Yes, but management has ruled out the name Taurus for these new cars," answered Smith.

> "Taurus happens to be an excellent name for these new cars," I remarked. "The bull conveys strength, power, and endurance. It's distinctive and memorable. Taurus sounds

like a well-built American car with mass-market appeal. Yes, it's aggressive, but it doesn't overpromise on what the car is capable of delivering."

"Do you really think it's that good of a name?" asked Smith.

"Absolutely!" I exclaimed. "It should be added to the finalist names for these new cars." Ford's management eventually adopted my recommendation to name the new product line "Taurus."

Ford's revolutionary Taurus sedan has ranked among the top three best-selling cars in America since it's introduction. For six years running, 1992 through 1997, Taurus was the No. 1 domestic selling car. Ford had the guts to take a risk by launching the Taurus, and it paid off handsomely to the tune of billions of dollars to the company and its shareholders. But more important, it has given a sense of pride to every blue- and white-collar Ford employee who played a part in this story of courage.

Lessons Learned

1. It takes knowledge and wisdom to find courage. Ford knew it had developed a breakaway product with Taurus cars. That made it easier for management to muster the courage to bet the Ford automotive ranch on the success of the Taurus. When you know in your gut that you haven't come close to developing a breakaway product, you will instinctively hold back on gambling part of your company's fortunes to roll out a major TV and print-ad campaign to support that product. In most cases, the product will have a short life span.

2. When your gut tells you that you have a WOW product but you hold back from betting big bucks on your convictions, then you may have missed the opportunity of a lifetime. At any rate, your competitors will be very happy.

DETERMINATION

Our lives have been enriched for the better thanks to many remarkable people who were determined to make their vision become a reality. The following quotes are meant to inspire us and to remind us that the naysayers out there have been proven wrong time and time again.

So we went to Atari and said, "Hey, we've got this amazing thing, even built with some of your parts, and what do you think about funding us? Or we'll give it to you. We just want to do it. Pay our salary, we'll come work for you." And they said, "No." So then we went to Hewlett-Packard, and they said, "Hey, we don't need you. You haven't got through college yet." (Steve Jobs on attempts to get Atari and HP interested in his and Steve Wozniak's personal computer)

We don't like their sound, and the guitar music is on the way out. (Decca Recording Company rejecting the Beetles, 1962)

If I had thought about it, I wouldn't have done the experiment. The literature was full of examples that said you can't do this. (Spencer Silver on the work that led to the unique adhesives for 3M Post-It Notepads)

The concept is interesting and well-formed, but in order to earn better than a "C," the idea must be feasible. (A Yale university management professor in response to Fred Smith's paper proposing a reliable overnight delivery service. Smith went on to launch FedEx.)

Louis Pasteur's theory of germs is ridiculous fiction. (Pierre Pachet, professor of physiology at Toulouse, 1872)

Drill for oil? You mean drill into the ground to try to find oil? You're crazy, (Drillers who Edwin L. Drake tried to enlist in his project to drill for oil in 1859. Drake [1819–1880] had given birth to the petroleum industry by striking oil at sixty-nine feet underground, the first true oil well. He neglected to patent his drilling invention, which would dominate the twentieth century—a pipe liner for the drilling hole. Sadly, he died a pauper.)

There is no reason why anyone would want a computer in their home. (Ken Olson, president, chairman, and founder of Digital Equipment Corp., 1977. As of mid-2000, three people are buying PCs for home use every second according to Microsoft. Oh, was Olson wrong!)

You can have vision, courage, and talent, but if you lack determination, your dream of hitting a brand slam with a new product or business venture will be just that—a dream. Apple's first attempt to market a mouse-activated desktop computer (called Lisa), which was far more user-friendly than Microsoft's DOS operating system, bombed. Had Steve Jobs not been determined to design, develop, and launch a user-friendly mouse-activated PC operating system (called Macintosh), the world of PC information processing as we know it might never have materialized. Microsoft's Windows 95 might never have been developed (it was a take-off on the Macintosh software, according to Apple), access to the World Wide Web might not be available today to hundreds of millions of people around the globe, and instant wealth made in Internet and technology stocks might never have happened. We should all write thank-you letters to Steve Jobs for making our lives easier and more productive.

Yes, there are examples in the marketplace where a company has stepped up to the plate and hit a brand slam for a new product or business venture. But more times than not, going for a brand slam has its unexpected challenges and strike outs. Only determination to succeed will get you and your team players around the bases to home plate.

Lessons Learned

1. Follow the example of Apple's CEO Steve Jobs: If at first you don't succeed, try, try, and then try a dozen times more until you do succeed.

2. The fuel that drives the determination to succeed for people like Jobs, Donald Trump, Steven Speilberg, Bijan, and Ralph Lauren, is an unwavering belief in a new product or business venture. It's that simple.

TALENT

Every company dreams of hitting a brand slam. Most will never achieve one, because it takes an incredible amount of talent. When you have talent, skill automatically comes with the gift. However, being skilled at something doesn't mean you have talent. Talent is about people who paint the picture they see like no one else can.

In the advertising business, talent is about people who create a big idea and then execute it in such a brilliant way that the commercial becomes forever etched in our minds. According to many in the media, the award for best commercial produced and aired in the twentieth century goes to Apple.

Apple Computer's now famous "1984" commercial aired only once during the 1984 Super Bowl game. The Macintosh commercial opened with shaved-head drones in gray clothing marching in step through an underground tunnel. Everything we see is in muted gray colors. The scene changes and we see a young athletic woman in a bright colored jersey and track shorts running with a sledge hammer in her hands. She enters into a meeting hall where the drones are now seated in rows—their eyes fixed on a giant screen where "big brother" is addressing them. She pivots, spins around three times and hurls the hammer toward the screen. Then the words "Apple Macintosh Has Arrived" appear on the screen. The Macintosh PC was never shown in the commercial, but the message was obvious to an estimated 100 million viewers: Apple's new Macintosh is going to change the way IBM does business. And history has shown that it did just that.

According to media insiders, Apple spent almost $1 million to air the sixty-second spot. This brand slam commercial created by Chiat/Day received so much industry acclaim and awards that it has been aired maybe one hundred times on national TV and worldwide cable channels at no media cost to Apple. Now that's WOW!

Michael Jordan is another example of how talent can lead to a brand slam. Without Michael Jordan's superior talent on the basketball court, there would be no Air Jordan, the sports footwear branded by Nike. And there would be no Nike stand-alone Michael Jordan brand for basketball shoes, cross-trainers, and apparel—all of which are marketed without the Nike swoosh. There also wouldn't be any JORDAN by Michael fragrance marketed by Bijan.

Here's yet another example of the marketing of a great talent. With the release of *Supernatural* by Arista in 1999, legendary guitarist Carlos Santana was on top of the charts again. Nominated that year for eleven Grammy awards and a best-album win at the American Music Awards, the world embraced Santana with a passion. If Santana has infused his music with a fresh energy and sensuous Afro-Cuban rhythms, it all comes down to one word—talent. Talent is behind the 30 million Santana albums sold and what has made this Rock 'n Roll Hall of Famer a global brand icon. Talent has produced the Santana music that touches the heart and soul of people, defies all geographic and cultural boundaries, and transcends languages. Did you know that five of the biggest record companies turned down Santana's *Supernatural* album, which then went on to become one of the most phenomenal success stories in music recording history?

Lessons Learned

1. You can have vision, courage, and determination, but if you lack the talent to bring people to their feet, your chances of hitting a brand slam are not good.

2. It takes talented people to create and execute breakaway campaigns. Advertising dollars without talent are worthless.

IT TAKES MUCH MORE

To hit a brand slam, you need vision, courage, determination, and talent. But that's not all. It takes smarts to know what marketing campaigns to use with consumers. Every new and emerging company automatically thinks of running TV spots and print ads to promote its product. But there are times when direct mail is more effective.

In 1993, AOL had 240,000 members in the United States. Looking for ways to build its customer base, Jan Brandt, marketing president of AOL, persuaded CEO Steve Case to do a direct mailing of AOL disks to consumers. The success of that mailing convinced both Brandt and Case to mail out AOL disks to tens of millions of Americans. Keep in mind that back then most people didn't know much about the Internet and that you needed a server provider like AOL to get online. Instead of trying to explain what it was like to surf the Internet via TV spots and print ads, AOL gave consumers free software to access the World Wide Web and the ability to surf sites around the globe. The end result? Membership skyrocketed.

AOL not only distributed its disks through a direct mailing, it broke new ground by attaching free disks in a protective bag in magazines, newspapers, and phone books. In airports, movie theaters, barber shops and beauty salons, as well as baseball stadiums and amusement parks, there were free AOL disks available in kiosks. AOL disks even showed up in product packaging, on CDs, and in cereal boxes. The goal to blanket America with AOL software on disks paid off—big time.

AOL hit a brand slam with millions of consumers by giving them a thirty-day trial period to go online and surf the Web. Not surprisingly, it's competitors followed suit and gave away free software and a similar thirty-day trial period. But AOL did it with more smarts than the other companies; no wonder it is No. 1 in the business.

Lesson Learned

Look at all of your options to create WOW in the marketplace.

6

BASES LOADED FOR A
BRAND SLAM

*If you've ever been to a ball game, the crowd lights up like a
1,000-watt halogen bulb when the bases are loaded. You
know your company's got a good chance of hitting a brand
slam when the people assigned to the project show up to work
at 4 A.M.*

To get the most out of this chapter, it's essential that I offer you a brief
overview of how brands evolved in America. They weren't called
"brands" back in the days when Thomas Jefferson, our country's third
president, traveled abroad not only for diplomatic reasons but to purchase
European-made products like French wines and cognacs, Spanish Madeira,
and Italian virgin olive oils. Yet, the producer's name appearing on the
wooden shipping cases and on each bottle inside is what we would call a
"brand name" today.

In the nineteenth century, if you shopped in a town's general store you
would find confections, herbs, spices, and dried fruits stored in nonbranded
large glass jars; flour, wheat, barley, and rice packaged in nonbranded cotton sacks; coffee beans housed in nonbranded burlap sacks; and blankets,
clothes, and candles all without any labels noting the maker's name. Most
of the items you purchased would be wrapped and tied in plain brown
paper bearing no mention of the store proprietor's name that sold you the
items. There were some exceptions, of course. For instance, if you browsed
about the store you might find double bars of Procter & Gamble's soap
with the name "Ivory" printed on the soap's paper wrapper, chocolate bars
with the name Hershey's, bottles of ketchup with the name Heinz printed

on the label, or rifles and boxes of gunpowder ammunition bearing the names Winchester, Remmington, or Smith & Wesson.

When merchants eventually stocked the same items made by different producers, it was obvious that each producer needed to differentiate its product from the competition. As more products entered the market—each one claiming to be the best product made—the maker's name came to stand for a promise of quality and satisfaction, or a brand that people could rely on. It was a prelude of what would eventually transform the general store into a fun shopping experience for the entire family. But it wasn't until the 1920s before brand-name products made their appearance in a noticeable number in flagship department stores located on America's big city avenues. Thus, the term *brand* gradually worked its way into the American lexicon.

First on Base Is a Great Brand Name

No single element in the making of a colossal brand is more important than the brand's name.

To hit a brand slam, the first runner to get on base is the brand's name. Don't settle for anything less than an "omnipowerful" brand name. It must be a *free agent* name, capable of being marketed on a broad range of products that bear no resemblance to the original product.[1] The brand's name is king in the marketing of any product, service, or business venture. In fact, highly memorable brand names like Amazon.com, Yahoo!, FedEx, Taurus, Pathfinder, Microsoft, Snickers, Skippy, Tide, Mr. Clean, Craftsman, Mach3, and Eveready are in themselves brand slams. If you disagree that a brand's name is king, then consider these sobering facts:

1. When you hit on the perfect brand name for a product, that name instantly sets the image positioning of that product for its life span in the marketplace. It also provides a measurable yardstick for evaluating anything that relates to that product. In contrast, if your brand name contains a word with poor phonetics or suggests inappropriate imagery, your product is doomed from day one to a life of changing advertising themes, vision statements, label and packaging designs, and image positioning strategies—all because the product's name was a poor choice.

---

1. The Omnipowerful Brand, *by Frank Delano. Chapters 1 through 6, explore the secrets to developing an omnipowerful brand name.*

2. Word of mouth is how most of us learn about products. Thus, the product's brand name is often the first statement of quality that piques our interest and makes us want to learn more.

3. Until you settle on a brand name, you can't launch a new product or business venture. How can you ask your advertising and PR agencies to develop effective campaigns to build consumer awareness for your new product or company if the brand name is missing from the picture? How do you instruct your design and communications people to come up with an award-winning logo and packaging design, product catalogues, technical literature, and an online Web site unless you have a brand name in place?

4. Some 95 percent of all products sold in America would not be identified by consumers if the product's brand name was removed from the package or label. Remove the name Dell from this computer manufacturer's boxes and you'll have instant brand anonymity. Brand identity is so important that Gateway, another computer manufacturer, uses a black cow-skin design on its white cartons. First, Gateway selected its founder's name and then it developed an image to go with it.

Proof That the Brand's Name Is King

Four decades ago, the buzzword heard in corporate boardrooms was "corporate identity." A new futuristic-looking company logo design was viewed by many CEOs as being the "silver bullet" for attaining revenue growth, attracting the attention of investors, and persuading the best minds at Ivy-league schools to join a company's ranks.

The 1960s also marked a decade when corporate logo designs were reinvented for industry giants including United Airlines, CBS, and IBM. Thirty years later, these logos and symbol designs seem to have plenty of high octane fuel left to propel them far into the twenty-first century and perhaps centuries beyond that. Keep in mind that the "cross" symbol denoting Christianity is now in its third millennium.

When I started my firm in 1974, I made it a practice of pinning up each new logo design that we created on the walls of our main conference room. After looking at these logos on an almost daily basis, several observations hit me: (1) The term *corporate identity* was misleading. What we were creating was an "umbrella brand identity" for companies. In essence, the names featured in these logos were brands first and corporate shorthand names second. (2) The best of these brand logos featured a word that communicated a memorable thought about the company's mission, its vision for the future, or the spirit propelling it to reach new plateaus. (3) The brand's name was more important than the design of the logo.

Here are three examples of umbrella brand names that communicate a powerful and memorable message:

- **Humana.** With just six letters, it speaks to the company's mission of providing lifesaving health care services to people regardless of their race, ethnicity, religious belief, or social ranking.
- **VISA.** With just four letters, it remind us that this company's credit card can be used anywhere in the world.
- **Amazon.com.** It sounds like an awesome and far-reaching Internet company—a competitive warrior in the e-commerce business. Amazon.com's CEO Jeff Bezos came up with the name thumbing through the "A" section of the dictionary. When he hit upon the name for the world's best known river, he stopped there.

On CNN's *Larry King Live,* the great American playwright Neil Simon told King that he must first conceive of his play's title before going on to write the play. "Why is that?" asked an inquisitive King.

Simon replied, "The title keeps me focused on what the play is all about." Likewise, the brand's name is meant to keep management focused on what the new product, service experience, or business venture is all about. When you do hit on a great one like Nissan's Pathfinder, it's obvious that the vehicle's design, engineering, and road handling performance should live up to the name's literal meaning.

Second on Base Is a Great Brand Logo

I don't care who's clicking the mouse, one hour at the computer will not buy you a logo design masterpiece.

Now that you've developed a great brand name, it's time to feature it in a breakaway logo design. Before you turn on your desktop computer and click on PhotoShop or another graphic software program, I have some sobering news to share with you about computer-generated logo designs.

Today's computer-literate graphic designers and art directors may have a difficult time creating a logo design on a piece of paper. You could say they have become slaves to the medium of computer design and are totally dependent on electronic art files. And if they can't find what they are looking for in these electronic files or on the Internet, chances are they will move on to something else. Remember, your brain's imagination can take you places that a computer has never been before.

When you're using a computer, it's very easy to get caught up in the typographical execution of a brand logo without realizing that the idea behind that design may be irrelevant or inappropriate to the brand's theme.

However, when you put your brand logo ideas down on paper you're more likely to focus on the relevancy of these ideas and not their execution. You're also training yourself to visualize and express your ideas with greater speed than you could ever accomplish by using a computer.

Computer-literate graphic designers and art directors typically begin the process of designing a logo by selecting a typeface that is available on the program they're working with (that's already limiting the logo design possibilities to the number of typefaces installed in the program). What they fail to realize is that all the popular typefaces used in advertising today were originally designed for book text, not logo designs. The designer of the typeface never thought his letter forms would exceed a cap height of seventy-two points in print. And he never thought that his typeface would be used for logo designs that might need to be enlarged to twenty-five feet in cap height for a lighted sign mounted at the top of a sixty-story building.

When a typeface like Garamond, Times Roman, or Century Gothic appears in text at ten point, we don't notice the inconsistencies and the imperfections in the type forms. We assume that the designer perfected every letter in his created typeface prior to its release for publication—wrong! Photo enlarge the complete alphabet of the typeface you have selected to three inches in cap height. After a few hours of visual study, you will see things you didn't see before when you were looking at the typeface in eighteen point. Here's what you are likely to find in most classic typefaces. The letters A, B, E, F, J, L, P, R, S, T, V, and Y are too condensed in form for use in a logo design. The letters C, D, G, H, I, K, N, O, Q, U, X, and Z are more regular in form and may need only minor optical adjustments for use in a logo design. The letters M and W are too extended in form for use with other vowel and consonant letters in a logo design.

To see for yourself what I am talking about, turn on your PC's Microsoft Word program and click on "Format" on the menu bar. Then click on "Font." Next, click on "Century Gothic, 72 point size" and look at the word *Century* on your monitor screen. Notice that the lower case letters t, r, and y look like twigs compared to the other fully formed letters. Assume that the logo design you're developing features the word *Century* and that you want to use this typeface. First, redraw these three letters to balance out the visual appearance of the word. That's where the art of typography comes into play, and your computer can't do it for you.

Since I have designed a number of logos for industry giants, I am often asked by graphic design students to name the typefaces I used to create these trademarks. They are shocked when I tell them it's not typeset; each letter in each logo is hand drawn. The lettering in some designs may look similar to certain classic typefaces, but they are all original works of art.

As a tool, the computer has liberated many young graphic designers and art directors from performing visual tasks by hand. On the downside, it's making them "visually illiterate" and keeping them from learning the art of creating type forms by hand. Sadly, the type director in the truest sense of that professional title is now on the endangered species list.

The great logo designs of the past century like CBS, IBM, Ford, and Mobil took the designers months to create. Compare any one of these award-winning designs with Amazon.com's logo and the latter looks like it was done in an hour. When I hit on a logo design that I believe is right on the money, I'll pin up the preliminary drawing on my studio wall and look at it for days, making mental notes of what needs to be reworked. It may take twenty or thirty revisions before I sign off on the final master artwork. Picasso spent more time studying his paintings in progress than he did applying paint to these canvases. There are no short cuts to achieving WOW in a logo design; the time you put into it is usually reflected in the end product.

Make Your Brand's Logo Your Own and Nobody Else's

Logo designs essentially fall into four groups: (1) A freestanding, distinctive typographical treatment of the company's brand name as reflected in the RCA logo. (2) An attendant graphic device linked with the company's brand name as reflected in the bars above and below the Visa logo. (3) A recognized graphic image linked with the company's brand name as reflected in the famous winglike "swoosh" Nike symbol. (4) A typographical treatment of the company's brand name housed in a memorable shape such as Kmart's "Big K" logo.

It's not a question of which of these logo types is superior to the others. It's more a question of which logo type best presents your company's umbrella brand, and which will make the most memorable impact on consumers. If your brand's name is highly distinctive like "Chanel,"—named after Coco Chanel, the company's founder and Paris' famed designer of women's couture fashion—then less is usually more in the creation of a brand logo. And that's precisely the direction Coco Chanel took, and the present day management continues to take, to keep the Chanel brand in a class of its own. The Chanel trademark features two interlocking Cs in a circle. The Chanel logo is simply a contemporary sans serif typeface. The brand's colors are gold, black, and white—a color palette that speaks to its premium-priced image. These trademark icons will remain timeless far into the twenty-first century.

Obviously, if your umbrella brand's name is a commonplace word or happens to be a familiar surname like McDonald's, then a memorable graphic image is essential to separate your brand from others using the same name. In the case of McDonald's, that graphic image is the famous Golden Arches. All you need is the "Golden Arches" symbol and "2 miles ahead" on a highway sign anywhere in the world and everyone will know that a McDonald's restaurant is just two minutes away. Now that's WOW!

Now look at the cartoonlike logo designs of some of the best-known dot-com companies, and you will see that they are quite different from that of the more traditional companies like IBM, Yahoo!, Webcrawler, Excite, and Mamma have logos that look like they belong on kids' chewing gum wrappers. On the other hand, AltaVista, America Online, Microsoft, and Intel's logos are more in keeping with the established IBM corporate look. In other words, they don't create shockwaves. The point is that no matter what logo you ultimately settle on, make it your own and nobody else's.

Lessons to Be Learned from Verizon's Logo Design

Verizon is the new company formed by the union of Bell Atlantic and GTE. In the company's logo, which features a nondescript sans serif typeface, the emphasis is on the "Z" letter; the "Z" appears in red while the other letters appear in black. When you look at the logo close-up, you have no problem reading the name Verizon. But when you see the logo at a distance, it's impossible to make out the "Z." So you're left wondering what "Veri on" means in Latin. When the logo appears in white on a darker background, all you see is "Veri on" because the red "Z" fades into the background color. It's hard to believe that management didn't see this.

It also seems that the press is not so taken with the name Verizon either. In *Crain's New York Business* (July 24, 2000, issue), reporter Steve Malange wrote:

> Bell Atlantic and GTE have picked the harsh and clumsy sounding Verizon as its new name . . . For the record, Verizon is a madeup word (you figured that out, I'm sure), constructed from "horizon" and the Latin word "veritas" or "truth." The notion I guess, is that the new company will be true, in the sense of credible and steady, and also forward looking. It's a lofty concept but a lousy word. The companies say they selected this out of 8,500 possibilities. I cringe to think what some of those others must have been.

Here's my personal critique of the name *Verizon*. It would have been better if Bell Atlantic and GTE selected a real word to represent the new company's values and vision for the future. The problem here is that we connect with the word *horizon* in the name, but we're left pondering what the first syllable "Ve" means. It's ironic that a communications company picked a new umbrella brand name that sends no clear message to the public.

When you're marketing "clear mobile" communications, and your company's name is not clearly understood to consumers, you look a little silly. In fact, the name "clear mobile" has a lot going for it, the message is clear and there's no chance of mispronunciation. I love it when chef Emeril Lagasse turns to his live TV audience and shouts, "Hey, it doesn't take a rocket scientist to figure this out." But then again, that's what I would expect from a company that named itself "Bell Atlantic." Talk about limiting. The company had to spend tens of millions in advertising dollars over the past decade to tell the world that its geographical reach went far beyond the Atlantic coastal region of America.

The most common mistake made by industry giants is a failure to recognize that the names they are testing rank in the league of tin, copper, and nickel. What's missing are the silver, gold, and platinum names. So a name worth only a nickel in terms of its communications value surfaces to the top in research testing and everyone jumps up and says, "We've got a winner." Wrong! What you have is a nickel.

The Power of Coca-Cola's Scripted Logo

In the mid-1990s, my firm did consumer research on some of the most recognized brand logos in the world. It consisted of four focus-group sessions with fifty people aged 18 to 35. Just for fun, we inverted the vowels in the Coca-Cola logo to read "Caco-Calo." Remarkable as it may sound, not one person during the daylong sessions picked up on the misspelling of this iconic brand name on eight-ounce soda cans. I can only conclude that they saw the familiar Coca-Cola scripted logo and assumed it was spelled "Coca-Cola."

THIRD ON BASE IS A GREAT WEB SITE

When you run a full-page ad in *Time*, there's no way for the consumer to interact with the medium. On a Web site, you can put consumers in charge and give them the opportunity to interact with your site. Right now, no other medium can do that, and that's what makes the Internet so awesome.

In 1994, I would have said an award-winning brand graphic design system is the third runner to get on base to set the stage for a brand slam. The power of the Internet has changed my thinking.

Why construct a Web site? The overriding reason is that people around the world can visit your site twenty-four hours a day, seven days a week. Any minute or hour of the day you can add or delete items, make copy changes, and upload new content to your site. In short, you control the content of your message to consumers at any given moment in time. That's a feat that has never been achieved in any other advertising mediums including TV, print, and billboard. Sure you can change the TV spot you're currently running on the networks, but you can't do it in five minutes.

In the fifteenth century when Johann Gutenberg was the first in Europe to print with movable type, he eventually put most book calligraphers out of work. With the invention of the e-brochure, the general commercial printing industry is going to shrink by the year 2005. If you're a small- to medium-size company, there is no reason why you need to produce a costly full-color brochure featuring your company's products or capabilities. This same information can now be found on your Web site at a fraction of the cost. Visitors to your site can print the pages and, in effect, have a color brochure about your company's product lines and other aspects of your business.

Tips on Producing a WOW Web Site

Despite all you've heard that the Web will be "the place" for twenty-four-hour shopping, it has got a long way to go before it truly becomes a great shopping browser for consumers. However, it's an excellent medium if you know what you want to buy, and it just may be the easiest way of ordering a product or service ever devised.

The key to creating a WOW Web site is to do more than just share information with others. Make your Web site a vehicle of persuasion in the same way that advertising and sales genius get us to buy something we don't need. The best Web sites have emotional impact. Unfortunately, far too many dot-com sites are information-driven, not persuasion-driven to sell brands. Here are some tips to create what I call "Web persuasion."

Your home page has to grab the visitor's attention with compelling graphics, photos, and jabbing headline punches. Review magazine covers of *Cosmopolitan, Talk, Maxim,* and *Business Week* for inspiration. If you start off with nothing more than a logo and a lengthy paragraph that runs over the screen's frame, you're going to turn off most visitors. The same is true if your home page shows only your brand's logo and a copy line that reads: "Click Here to Enter Our Site." What's with the teasing? This is your chance to hook readers; otherwise, they will head back to a search engine site like Yahoo.com to click on one of your competitor's sites. Again, newsstand magazine covers highlight topics designed to get the public's attention. "Is the Bull Market Over?" That was the headline on the cover of *Newsweek* when the Nasdaq lost 25 percent of its market value ($2 trillion) during the week of April 10 to April 14, 2000. A headline in *Cosmopolitan* such as "Ten things that newly made millionaires want in a relationship," is a natural hook for women who want to meet or keep Mr. Bucks.

Avoid too many graphic icons and definitely don't use decoy icons, which are symbols that when you click on them, nothing happens. What works best on a home page are photos of products or people that you can click on and get the story. Visit Nike's home page (www.nike.com) to see what I am talking about. If you do use icons, they should serve to help visitors navigate around your site's pages. Cyberspace is all about the speed that you can travel to get information around the world on almost any topic. Your site should be designed to get information fast.

Links to other Web sites can be enormously helpful. If you visit my firm's site (www.frankdelano.com), you can point-and-click "Purchase Frank Delano's books." Within seconds, you will be connected to Amazon.com's site. (This is *not* an ad!) Visit the General Motors site (www.gm.com), and you'll see a masterpiece in how they link GM's car divisions and products from one core site.

Use white or a light background color if you want visitors to print out a copy of your site's pages. Text reversed out of a dark-colored background may look dramatic on your PC screen, but it will be difficult to read on a laser printout. Visit Bang & Olufsen's Web site (www.bang-olufsen.com) and you'll see the advantages of using click-on photos and an off-white background for printing page copies.

The best way to plan and design an effective Web site is to visit other companies' sites that have been given thumbs up from interactive media critics. *Advertising Age* publishes a regular "Cybercritique" column. It does a good job exposing the best and the worst Web sites and banner ads. If this is your first venture into interactive media, the sites listed in "Cybercritique" will give you a good idea of what works and what doesn't.

When visitors come to your site, make it easy for them to send email to people in your organization who deal with product sales, after-sales service support, media relations, employee recruitment, and stock ownership plans. After all, the Web serves as a direct, ongoing, interactive connection between people using this medium around the world. If your site is no more than a home page, think of it as a listing in the *Yellow Pages*. The power of the Internet is not working for your company if email addresses, phone and fax numbers, and postal addresses remain a mystery to visitors.

Now Hit the Brand Slam

Once the bases are loaded, you're ready to go for that winning brand slam—be it a breakaway marketing or advertising campaign, or the launch of a breakthrough new product. Remember the importance of a brilliant execution of whatever it is that you're introducing to the public and the media.

In the game of brand slams, you need to have in your dugout:

1. A public relations team that's committed to working around the clock to get reporters, desk editors, journalists, and TV producers excited about your news story.

2. A manufacturing, distribution, and a dealership network that's committed to backing your new campaign or product 110 percent.

3. A turbo-charged sales force that lives and breathes your company's flagship brand. Remember, when a sales representative speaks to a customer, that person *is* your brand at the moment.

7

ADVERTISING THAT HITS A BRAND SLAM

Advertising should be fun. When you're having fun, you are more likely to do your best and boldest work. Conversely, if you are fearful, rigid, or simply bored, that will show in your work. Just look at the best agencies. You'll find cultures that encourage enthusiasm, freethinking, risk-taking, lively debate, and pure enjoyment of the business we're in.
  Rick Boyko, chief creative officer at Ogilvy & Mather North America.

QUALITIES OF GREAT ADVERTISING

In my book *The Omnipowerful Brand,* I review seven identifiable qualities of great brand advertising. I've added these points here because you need to know them if you want to hit a brand slam campaign. Keep in mind that these identifiable and wholly predictable qualities go beyond my own experiences of what works and doesn't work in advertising; they incorporate the thinking of some of the best minds in the ad business.

1. **A Big Idea.** Nothing else is so important to hitting a brand slam advertisement than a big idea that captures the product's most compelling story. Does the idea go beyond execution? Does it show insight into your product? Benton & Bowles' ad agency said it best more than two decades ago: "Before you approve any

advertisement, ask yourself if it really has a big idea and if that idea emerges clearly, emphatically, and singlemindedly."[1]

2. **A Brand Focus.** When you advertise your product, don't forget to also sell your company's umbrella brand to consumers. A product's integrity and after-sale service support usually are backed by the manufacturer. If your Walkman breaks, you would expect Sony to make good on the product's warranty, not the brand Walkman.

3. **A Theme Line.** A memorable advertising theme line can rocket your brand off the charts. When Microsoft launched Windows 95, it caught the world's attention with the ad theme line "Start Me Up," inspired by the Rolling Stones' hit record title. The challenge, of course, is to present your genuine selling idea in a memorable set of words. When you hit on a great one, I recommend that you feature it in all media and on your Web site's home page.

4. **Relevance.** If your advertising is remembered but your brand is forgotten, then you are advertising a big *creative* idea, not a big *brand* idea. Or special effects that have no relevancy to your product's genuine selling idea may be stealing the show. Choosing celebrities who have no logical connection with your brand, and other irrelevancies can add up to a costly mistake.

5. **Original.** Is your campaign fresh and original, or is it a recycled concept of somebody else's advertising? Benton & Bowles correctly said, "Don't run the risk of being mistaken for your competitor. Demand a campaign that is all your own."

6. **Showing.** Nothing works harder to sell your brand than a demonstration of your product's superiority, especially if such a demonstration speaks to your product's most compelling story. Gillette's Mach3 TV spots show graphically how its revolutionary three-blade razor system can't be bested by any twin-blade razor in the marketplace.

7. **Credibility.** If your campaign over-promises, the selling idea will sound a false note to target buyers. Great ads push the credibility factor to the edge, but they don't cross the line.

TELL THE PRODUCT'S MOST COMPELLING STORY

David Ogilvy correctly instructed his clients: "If you have news to deliver, deliver it." In short, your advertisement should tell the most compelling

---

1. *Benton & Bowles is now called D'Arcy, Masius, Benton & Bowles. The ad agency's headquarters are in New York.*

story about your brand name product to consumers. That story usually falls into one of three themes: the product's essence, the product's uniqueness, or the product's spirit. If you select a theme that is not focused on your product's most compelling story, you will have missed a chance to go for an advertising brand slam.

Actually, it's not that difficult to determine what is the most compelling story to tell about your product in your campaign. If your product has a unique selling proposition or a unique product feature that no competitive product can match, then that's the news to deliver. If your product, by its very uplifting spirit, will enhance the buyer's lifestyle or change her perceptions of herself in a positive way, then that's what you should highlight. If the story is the sum and substance of the product, then that's your hook.

Sometimes there's more than one compelling story to tell consumers. For example, "a retro-1940s hot rod with a high-racked roof line" separates Chrysler's new PT Cruiser from anything else on the road today. Yet another unique selling proposition of this vehicle is its twenty-six different seating and back shelf arrangements. To leave out the latter point in TV spots would be a big mistake. Here's another way to determine if you've made the right theme call. Does the message you have selected speak to the overriding reason that persuaded you to invest a fortune to bring this product into the marketplace? If so, the ball is in your agency's court to come up with a big idea that fully captures your product's most compelling story.

Remember, great ad campaigns have this in common: They tell a compelling story about the product or the service experience in simple language that people can understand.

A MEMORABLE IMAGE THAT'S ALL YOUR OWN

When you find or invent a memorable advertising image (symbol or character) that's all your own, you're hitting a brand slam. Some of these images bear the honor of being America's most trusted brand icons. For kids, it's Ronald McDonald, Tony the Tiger, the Quaker Oat's Man, Aunt Jemima, Mr. Peanut, Charlie the Tuna, and Elsie the Cow. For homemakers, it's the Maytag man, Mr. Clean, Mr. Whipple, Betty Crocker, and Uncle Ben's. For Colombian coffee aficionados, it's Juan Valdez standing next to his mule. For owners of battery-operated devices, it's the Energizer pink bunny. For car repair and maintenance, it's Mr. Good Wrench. For antacid relief, it's Speedy.

Sprint came up with a brilliant idea to communicate to consumers the sound clarity of its fiber optic telephone lines compared to the conventional lines used by its No. 1 rival AT&T. In its TV spots, a person on the other end of the phone hears a pin drop on a table next to a phone handset. A simple hemming pin has since taken its place as Sprint's long-distance network symbol. In fact, you can switch to Sprint by just calling 1-800-pin-drop. Now that's what I call marketing smarts.

Coca-Cola's creative geniuses invented yet another memorable brand image to add to the soft drink maker's stockpile of advertising icons. Coke's computer-animated polar bear family enjoys gulping down the world's No. 1 dark-carbonated brew. The advertised message comes through loud and clear that a cold bottle of Coke is a real thirst quencher.

TOP TEN BRAND SLAM CAMPAIGNS

Here they are, my top ten picks of the most memorable ad campaigns of the twentieth century. What do they have in common? Each ad theme captures the essence of the product's appeal in just a few simple words.

1. **Volkswagen's "Think small."** I can't think of a better way to say, "here's a car that's easy on your wallet, easy to maneuver, and easy to park in tight spaces" than Volkswagen Beetle's "Think small" ad campaign.

2. **Wendy's "Where's the beef?"** Everyone has seen those misleading commercials that show a good-size juicy burger inside a big sesame seed bun. That point was reverberated in our heads in Wendy's "Where's the beef?" TV spots that criticized its competitors for shilling small-size burgers.

3. **Diet Coke's "Just for the Taste of It."** You want to cut down on soft drink calories, but you don't want to cut down on taste and enjoyment. It's hard to come up with a better ad theme line than Diet Coke's "Just for the taste of it."

4. **McDonalds' "You deserve a break today."** You're a mom or dad with three kids and lunch at a family restaurant is far beyond your household budget. Yet, you need an escape from the daily grind. McDonald's ad campaign "You deserve a break today" struck a chord with millions of moms and dads.

5. **Smith Barney's "They make money the old-fashioned way—they earn it."** Selling stock brokerage services to affluent people is a tough sell. The ad theme line, "They make money the old-fashioned way—they earn it," scored a brand slam for Smith Barney with investors unhappy about the attention they were getting from their current stock brokerage firm.

6. **Nike's "Just do it."** Nike wanted to capture the spirit of sports in a simple ad theme line. Solution: "Just do it."

7. **Noxzema's "Take it off."** I have a confession to make. I was hooked on Gillette's Foamy aerosol shaving cream. But I switched to the Noxzema brand when I heard that sexy Scandinavian-

looking blonde actress say in TV spots, "Take it off, take it all off." I still buy Noxzema's shaving cream today, even though these commercials stopped airing decades ago—that's the lasting power that a brand slam advertisement can have on consumers.

8. **Life cereal's "He likes it."** How do you get children to eat a high-fiber nutritional bran cereal that appeals mostly to adults? You have two older boys test the product with their three-year-old brother "Mikey" to get his reaction. "He likes it!" sent the message to kids that they were missing out on Life cereal's enjoyable taste. It also took an obscure cereal product to national stardom. If the child actor who played Mikey is still getting residuals from these TV spots that aired for more than twelve years, he's got to be a very happy man now.

9. **L'Oréal's "I'm worth it."** When you're selling a do-it-yourself permanent hair color product that retails for close to $10 a pop, your advertising has to convey attributes like resiliency and new body, protection against hair damage, and rich color with maximum gray protection. All of that is conveyed in just three memorable words, "I'm worth it" by L'Oréal.

10. **Army's "Be all that you can be."** The U.S. Army wanted to change the public's perception of the caliber and spirit of the men and women who serve to protect our country. "Be all that you can be" did just that and much more.

In a *Dateline* NBC TV interview, reporter Maria Shriver asked media mogul Ted Turner in one word or another what makes for success in business. After much prodding on Shriver's part, Turner replied, "Early to bed, early to rise, work your ass off, and advertise." Quite frankly, I don't think even the legendary ad man David Ogilvy could have said it better than Turner. If your brand is out of sight, it's out of mind with consumers.

BREAKAWAY ADVERTISING

Here are a few of my favorite brand slam commercials and an outdoor sign that all illustrate the power of brand slam advertising. These spots are clever, moving, and inspirational—we haven't seen anything like them before.

No One Does It Better Than Mercedes-Benz

In the automotive industry, when there's no big advertising idea or a genuine selling proposition for the vehicle, the advertiser's commercial is like vanilla ice cream. How many times have we seen ad spots where a manufacturer's car is being driven at high speeds along a winding coastal roadway or over a parched desert earth? No other automaker's commercials have done a better job in keeping its flagship brand and product heritage alive in consumers' minds than Mercedes-Benz. One of its best ad themes was "Falling in Love Again," created by Lowe & Partners, New York, which aired in 1998. The TV spot opens with archival footage from the 1950s and continues on to the present day as we see people racing, driving, building, polishing, or just admiring their Mercedes-Benz cars. In every scene people are singing "Falling in Love Again." It's a brilliant reminder of our love affair with Mercedes-Benz cars even if we never owned one before.

The message of this commercial is powerful: The Mercedes-Benz brand is steeped in traditional values, and it is known for building cars with a unique combination of luxury, high performance, styling, and heritage. At the same time, the Lowe commercial speaks to passion, prestige, romance, and fun. Advertising doesn't get any better than this.

Monster.com Turns to Kids to Hit a Brand Slam Ad Campaign

This is one more example of how hitting brand slams has little to do with planning, planning, and more planning. Sometimes you just have to step up to the plate and smack one out of the ball park. Monster.com's objective was to become the Web site destination for anyone thinking about a job change. After the company had bought Super Bowl ad slots (at big bucks) to launch Monster.com, the newly recruited Mullen ad agency in Wenham, Massachusetts, had about seven weeks to develop a breakaway commercial. There was simply no time for planning strategies or testing campaign concepts with consumers. There was only time to conceive and produce a commercial.

The campaign focusing on the emotions of kids talking about what they want to be when they grow up hit a nerve with millions of unhappy employees. "When I grow up . . ." won the *Advertising Age* best of show commercial for 1999, and a 2000 EFFIE award from New York's American Marketing Association. Monster.com went on to become one of the most successful dot-com launches of the year, according to the AMA. Before Monster.com's spots aired during the Super Bowl, traffic to its site was running at about 1.5 million visitors per month. For the remainder of 1999, it averaged 2.5 million visitors per month. According to Monster.com's CEO, Jeff Taylor, traffic is running at 4 million visitors per month as of June 2000.[2] That's because Monster.com's advertising continues to be smart, creative, and universal.

---

2. *Source:* Advertising Age.

GM Calls on "Batman" to Pitch OnStar

Tie an icon figure like Batman to a car's satellite-link communications system answered by an actual human being, not a voice-recorded message, and you've got nothing short of a megahit in advertising. The cinematography of this commercial is right out of a Hollywood-produced Batman movie. We see Batman jumping off of a tall building with his cape acting as a parachute. He lands into the driver's seat of his Batmobile. He ignites the jet engine and "low fuel" lights up on the dashboard. He touches the bright blue OnStar button on the dashboard, and we hear an operator ask, "How can I help you, Batman?"

"I'm low on jet fuel," answers Batman.

"No problem," replies the OnStar operator. "Just two miles ahead on your left is a jet fuel station."

"Thanks," says Batman as we watch the Batmobile blast off.

Energizer Looks to "The King" to Sell Its Batteries

The commercial opens and we see an attendant seated inside a gas station booth. The walls are decorated with Elvis memorabilia. A vintage tailfin bluish-purple Cadillac convertible pulls up to an island pump. We can't see the driver's face as he fills up the Caddy's tank. But he's wearing one of Elvis' signature white and rhinestone studded Las Vegas outfits. "It's 'The King,'" says the attendant. He comes out of the booth to snap a photo. When he aims his camera, we finally see a side view of Elvis' face. To the shock of the attendant, the camera's batteries are dead. Elvis drives off and we hear a voice-over actor say, "Should have used Energizer batteries."

Mach3 Cuts a Winning Path for Gillette

Nothing beats a great brand name to introduce the most significant product breakthrough in its category in a generation. Mach3 is a radical new shaving system invented by the folks at Gillette. BBDO New York's campaign for this new razor focuses on the ad theme "The Best a Man Can Get." Through an explosive communications program, Mach3 rocketed to the No. 1 razor spot on the market and even surpassed the incredibly successful Gillette Sensor product.

"When You're Here, You're Family" Promises the Olive Garden

Grey Advertising was handed a real challenge: Stop the erosion of traffic and sales at the Olive Garden in the face of fierce competition and make it "hot" again. The creative people at Grey came up with an emotionally compelling reason to eat at the Olive Garden that went beyond good Italian food at affordable prices. In the commercials, we see Italian relatives seated around a large table enjoying the hospitality and the variety of pasta dishes served at the Olive Garden. "Here's a place where you're going to feel just like family" is the promise made in these spots.

"Boyd House for Sale" Lifts Century 21's Brand Image

We all know that the charged-up advertising and promotional campaigns seen in these spots to announce "Boyd House for Sale" are purely fictional. Yet, this commercial created by Lowe & Partners hits a brand slam with people who realize that buying and selling a home is not perfect, but that an understanding real estate company like Century 21 can make a difference.

GE Profile Performance's Gourmet Dad

In this amusing commercial created by BBDO New York, a dad gets carried away and cooks up one gourmet dish after another on a GE Profile Performance kitchen range. When his daughter comes into the kitchen, she sees a spread of Epicurean foods on the table that's utterly mind-boggling. "Dad," she says, "I thought we were just having breakfast." The commercial revitalized GE's range business and reversed a long-term downward trend in GE consumer brand commitment.

The Bronx Zoo Brings the Congo to a School Girl

The spot opens and we see a young school girl attracted by the sound of something moving in what appears to be dense jungle bushes. Suddenly, a large ape appears and comes toward the girl. Instead of running away, she moves toward the creature. When she takes another step forward, the tip of her nose flattens out and we realize she's protected by a glass wall separating her from the ape. It's one of the most powerful advertisements I've seen in a long time. The funny thing is: Not one spoken word is uttered in this commercial. Just the words "Bronx Zoo Congo" appear at the end. This commercial rates a double WOW in my book. The people responsible for conceiving and producing these Bronx Zoo Congo spots deserve special recognition from the mayor of New York.

Best Outdoor Ad Sign Goes to Yahoo!

If you're driving along San Francisco's James Lick Skyway on an approach to the Bay Bridge, you'll see a Yahoo! outdoor sign that brings to mind those garish Holiday Inn neon signs from the 1960s. Created by Black Rocket, San Francisco, the sign says "A nice place to stay on the Internet," referring to the big purple Yahoo! name above. An attached box at the bottom of the sign reads, "Free email, all U can eat buffet." And in keeping with the character of a motel sign, the word "Vacancy" is at the top of the sign blaring at you. This outdoor ad won a 1999 "Best Award" from *Advertising Age*.

A BRAND BLUNDER

Taco Bell's Talking Chihuahua Gets a Pink Slip

Taco Bell has struggled for decades to come up with a breakaway advertising campaign. It hit pay dirt when it created the little Chihuahua dog with his bigger-than-life ears and south-of-the-border dubbed-in voice. In advertising, the best way to get your message across is with a celebrity. Some of the best celebrities have been animals (including invented ones like the Energizer pink bunny), not movie stars. In perhaps the shortest time span in advertising history, Taco Bell's talking Chihuahua achieved a brand icon status with millions of consumers. His very appearance in a TV commercial or print ad immediately brought to mind Taco Bell and its Mexican-style tacos, bean burritos, nachos, gorditas, chalupas, Mexican pizza, and salsa.

So what did the marketing geniuses at Taco Bell do after they hit a brand slam with the talking Taco Bell Chihuahua? They pulled the plug on the little dog on July 19, 2000, claiming lagging sales at its restaurants. That's as bad as Kellogg's Corn Flakes firing Tony the Tiger. On the then *Regis and Kathie Lee Live* show, cohost Regis Philbin remarked, "Guess what? They dropped the Taco Bell dog. I can't imagine why they'd do that." Similar sentiments were echoed that day by all of the news network anchors.

Let me say it one more time: Never mess with a brand icon unless you've come up with something that's going to create WOW in the marketplace. Once consumers develop an emotional loyalty to an advertised brand icon, especially an animal, they don't like it when it's taken away from them. Taco Bell's management is about to learn the hard way what RCA's management learned in the late 1960s when it abandoned the famous RCA Nipper dog for a contemporary logo design. The consumer and employee backlash went on for two decades.

I recall visiting an RCA factory back in the early 1970s. The employees hung a big flag on the factory wall with this message: "Bring Back Nipper." Their voice was finally answered by a new management regime many years later. Taco Bell, if you're listening, 50 million people living in America own dogs. "It's easy for a fast food company to blame its ad agency's campaign for lagging sales. The real problem at Taco Bell is that its homogenized Mexican-style meals are about as appetizing as the food served on a discount airline," said a restaurant chain top executive who requested anonymity.

WHEN PRODUCT OR SERVICE
EXPERIENCE GETS IN THE WAY

U.S. Airways' New Spots Lack Credibility

One recent TV commercial airing for U.S. Airways starts with a woman talking to a terminal ticket agent. "I've been away in Germany for two years, what's new?" she asks. He ticks off a number of changes like new terminals, new aircraft, new airplane interiors, sleeper seats, new frequent flyer clubs, and new destinations to European cities. We see behind him a new U.S. Airways symbol—it's a graphic takeoff of the American flag. Then we catch a look at a jumbo jet painted with the company's new graphic identity scheme. "Well, it seems like you've done a lot," she says with a look of approval on her face.

What's wrong with this ad's selling pitch? We've heard it before a dozen times by other airline companies and little has changed in the actual service experience. These U.S. Airways spots don't address the real gripes of flyers like lost luggage, overbooking, delays, long lines, unappetizing food, no crew to fly the plane, and an indifferent customer service attitude. In short, it's the quality of the people and a commitment to excellence that make all the difference in the airline service business, not slapping leather on airplane seats and stamping a new symbol on everything in sight. When will the airlines get the message?

This Product's Side Effects Include a 90 Percent Chance of Coma Leading to Death

With the U.S. Food and Drug Administration's (FDA) relaxed rulings on pharmaceutical companies being able to advertise directly to consumers, the pill makers and their agencies have been having a field day. Prescription drug advertising has become one of the fastest growing segments of the ad business. When you look at the top ten TV network category spenders, prescription medicines ranked fifth with $521.9 million in 1999, and media buying is up 33.3 percent from 1998.[3] Add print, radio, Internet, and direct-mail advertising to the picture and we're talking about a staggering $1.9 billion in advertising spending.

Thanks to heavy TV advertising spending, ethical brands like Viagra, Paxil, Celebrex, Vioxx, Lamisil, Prilosec, and Claritin have become household names.

But unlike the advertising of consumer products, the FDA requires that drug makers inform the public in their TV spots of the product's potential side effects based on clinical studies. So, how does an ad agency deal with this issue?

---

3. Source: Competitive Media Spending.

It hires an actress with a soothing voice to voice-over the list of the unpleasant or even harmful side effects of the product in the spots. In one such spot the scene suddenly shifts to six adorable golden retriever puppies frolicking about as the voice-over actress begins informing us of the drug's side effects.

Now here's a parody on a commercial touting a therapeutic drug for social anxiety panic: As the spot comes to a close we're convinced that this drug is an effective treatment for the disorder. Then, the voice-over actress says: "Vaxilmol may not be for everyone. People taking Vaxilmol have experienced vomiting, diarrhea, sexual impotence, facial acne, body rash, hair loss, foul breath, fainting spells, excessive perspiration, trembling, a loss of bladder control, numbness of the hands, and swelling of the feet and ankles." Nothing here that a person experiencing social anxiety panic attacks can't handle, don't you think? Even though the reassuring voice of the actress convinces thousands of people that the drug's benefit outweighs the possible side effects, ads like these have a tough row to hoe to hit a brand slam.

WHEN THE AD ITSELF PREVENTS A BRAND SLAM

A Helicopter in Pursuit of an Oldsmobile Intrigue Doesn't Fly

Not one Oldsmobile Intrigue commercial that I've seen since the car's launch in 1988 explains to target buyers what this car is all about, and why you should own it. In a recent Intrigue TV spot (aired in June 2000), we see a helicopter pursuing the car as it exits a highway. Inside the moving sedan, a woman in the front passenger seat says to the driver, "Honey, there's that helicopter again." As the car eventually comes to a stop, she says, "Some telemarketers never give up, do they?"

Now you tell me what is the big selling idea behind this commercial? Don't worry, I don't know either. The story line in the spot says nothing about why you should buy this car or why a helicopter is in pursuit of it. What does the reference to a telemarketer have to do with motivating you to buy this four-door sedan that sells in the mid-$20,000 range? Oldsmobile's ad agency needs to come up with a big idea for the Intrigue and the only way to do that is to answer this question: "Why is this car being manufactured?" If it can answer that question in a one-line sentence, it has identified a selling idea for the car's ad campaign. Great campaigns are not vague and complex; they're clear and simple, and we come away remembering what the product or the experience means to us.

But time is running out for Oldsmobile to create an Intrigue TV spot that's a brand slam. On December 12, 2000, the General Motors Corporation announced that it would gradually phase out its Oldsmobile division over the next few years. According to the *New York Times*, Oldsmobile dealers decried GM's decision to shut down the 103-year-old division, saying that Oldsmobile had gone off track by abandoning older buyers of full-size cars in an unsuccessful attempt to win over younger, better-educated customers.

Big Deal, "M&M's Plain" Will Now Be Called "M&M's Milk Chocolate Candies"

The Mars company started modestly when Frank C. Mars, a candy sales-man, and his wife started their first candy-making operation in the kitchen of their Tacoma, Washington, home in 1911. Almost three decades later, Forest E. Mars founded M&M Limited and began making the now famous M&M's Plain Chocolate Candies.

M&M's Plain and Peanut Chocolate Candies are identified by the fa-miliar "M" on their unique sugar shells. For some unknown reason, Mars announced to the world's press that "M&M's Plain," as noted on the prod-uct's packaging for sixty years, would be changed to "M&M's Milk Choco-late Candies." To spend millions developing, producing, and buying the media slots to air a TV commercial announcing this product description change is comical. Give me a break. Everyone knows that M&M's Plain are milk chocolate candies without the peanuts. In an age when brand man-agers are looking to find a single word to describe their product to con-sumers, Mars has gone from one word to three words.

When Matt Lauer noted that the word *Plain* would no longer appear on M&M's candy wrappers, his cohost Katie Couric on NBC's *Today* show said, "I guess the marketing guys at Mars have nothing better to do with their time." This commercial, in my opinion, struck out before it was even aired.

It only makes sense to change the name, brand theme line, packaging, graphics, and color of a legendary American brand icon when what you're changing to is unquestionably a marketing coup. If it's just change for the sake of change, as it is in this case, you're only going to confuse consumers. Consider this scenario to make my point: "Sir, I'd like a big bag of M&M's Plain," asks a woman in her fifties to the counter salesperson at a Broadway theater house.

"Sorry Ma'am, M&M's stopped making Plain, but we do have M&M's Milk Chocolate Candies," he tells her.

"Well, in that case, I'll take a big Hershey's bar!"

Sprint's 1,000 Weekends TV Spots Are an Exercise in Distraction

I've had to suffer through watching these commercials a dozen times, and I am still trying to figure out what is the selling proposition offered in Sprint's 1,000 weekends. The spots open and we see the TV actress Sela Ward swiveling her hips in a tight pair of glittering pants while mumbling something about Sprint weekend minutes over the sound of the music track. As she's kicking up her feet to a lively beat, the camera zooms in on her sexy figure. Of course, this beautiful woman is not distracting us from listening to Sprint's advertised offer, right? Wrong. Here's a classic example of an advertiser picking a TV personality who has no logical connection with the advertised brand. The celebrity then becomes more of a distraction than a selling point, and that can turn out to be a costly mistake.

THE TROUBLE WITH PRODUCT COMPARISONS

They say in advertising that nothing works harder than a demonstration of your product's superiority over a competing product, especially in television. Let's face it, every advertiser is out to hit a brand slam and gain market share for their products. After all, competition is what makes America so great. So it's logical that an advertiser is going to want to see its product presented in a better way than the comparison product shown in the same spot. However, an agency that pushes the envelope too far to make the competitor's product look inferior will only make the advertiser look bad in the minds of consumers watching the TV spot.

The next time you see a comparison product commercial, notice how the advertiser's product is staged differently from the competitor's product to gain an advantage. A recent TV spot for new Liquid Tagamet is a good example.

Tagamet Spots Make Mylanta and Maalox Look Like Yesteryears' Antacids

The commercial opens and we see a male actor in his mid-thirties with a full head of black hair dressed in a smart-looking black golfer's shirt. He tells us that over-the-counter Tagament now comes in liquid form for quick and effective acid relief. Then he goes on to tell us that we would have to take four spoonfuls of the other liquid antacids to get the same relief from one spoonful of Tagament. Meanwhile, we see a bald, overweight man in his mid-fifties. The man's image is repeated four times, and in each image he's dosing four spoonfuls of a popular antacid. Well, four times four adds up to sixteen, not four spoonfuls of Mylanta or Maalox (which would equal one spoonful of Liquid Tagament). When we see an attractive woman dosing one spoonful of the advertiser's product, she's not repeated four times taking the single dosage.

The Tagament spokesperson appears in gray tones denoting neutrality, while the four repeat images of the man dosing a competitive liquid antacid appear in yellows and reds denoting an acidlike condition. Now I ask you, was this TV spot deliberately staged to present Mylanta and Maalox to consumers in a far less favorable light than Tagament? You had better believe it was. The agency who developed this Tagament spot pushed the envelope right to the edge, but it did it in such a devious way that many consumers will not necessarily pick up on the staging differences and yell foul play.

Fantastik Takes a Cheap Shot at 409 All Purpose Cleaner

The spot opens and we see a homemaker testing 409 and Fantastik to clean up a grease stain. Two Fantastik police officers rush in just in time to rescue her from the 409 product. Now talk about negative product staging, the female Fantastik officer picks up the 409 plastic container by the tip of its spray head and makes a facial gesture as if she's holding a big dead rat by the tail. She places the 409 bottle in a crime scene plastic bag. What's missing in this commercial is proof that Fantastik is a superior cleaner to 409. I can't speak for other consumers, but this commercial sold me on 409. Perhaps it's because the folks who created the Fantastik spot forgot that people don't like it when an advertiser takes a cheap shot at its competitor's product.

Egg Wave's TV Spot Is an Example of What Not to Do

The TV spot opens and the voice-over actress is pitching how simple it is to make perfectly cooked eggs every time in your microwave using the Egg Wave. The product, which looks like a large egg-shaped cup with a lid, is demonstrated in color over and over again. Then she tells us that with Egg Wave you're not cooking with all that unhealthy grease. The scene switches and we see, in black and white footage, two eggs frying in one inch of gritty-looking cooking oil in a large stove-top pan that looks like a 25-cent garage sale special. Give me a break. Who fries their eggs in one inch of fat? A consumer with any intelligence would see that this advertiser is not to be trusted.

Dot-Com Super Bowl Ads

Lee Weinblatt, who runs an advertising research company that tries to figure which TV spots are effective, has found that even the most amusing ads do not necessarily accomplish their goal.

In an ABC news segment *Deconstructing Hype,* which aired December 22, 2000, reporter John Stossel noted that during the Super Bowl, many of us talked about the artsy ads that ran. But sometimes you could not tell what the ads were for.

In Stossel's interview with Weinblatt, the researcher said, "There was a big deal about the dot-coms that were on the Super Bowl. According to

Weinblatt, "twelve of the people he polled liked the dot-com commercials best. Nine out of those 12 dot-coms either went out of business or got rid of their [advertising] agency," he noted.

Stossel added, "So even the experts on hype can't be sure that you'll buy what that hype . . ."

Brand slam ads are not about hype. They're about delivering a memorable and convincing commercial message about the product or service experience.

LESSONS LEARNED

1. Your ad campaign is not clever. It's not funny. It's not poignant. It's not inspirational. It's not motivating. It's not surprising. It's not daring. What do you do? It's simple: Fire your ad agency and get one that knows how to conceive and produce commercials for your product that will hit a nerve with consumers.

2. Get out of the planning, planning, and more planning mode and get into the "big idea" mode. An ad campaign that lacks a genuine selling proposition will stall and prove to be a costly media experience.

3. Your ad theme line should capture the essence of the product's appeal to consumers in just a few simple words. If it doesn't, tell your agency to go back to the drawing board.

4. Nothing beats a great brand name to inspire a winning ad campaign.

5. Never change or retire an advertised brand icon unless you have something to replace it with that will create more "WOW."

6. Comparison product TV spots that aren't believable are the kiss of death.

8

SLOGANS THAT HIT
A BRAND SLAM

*If consumers get nothing out of your commercial, at least let
them come away remembering your brand's slogan.*

An *ad theme* like Wendy's "Where's the beef?" speaks to the message
delivered in the advertised campaign. A *brand slogan* (also called a
brand catchphrase, brand theme line, or *brand tag line*) such as GE's
"We bring good things to life" is aimed at reminding consumers of what the
company and its products are all about. This is true regardless of whether
the ad campaign appears in print or on TV.

While even the best ad campaign themes have on average a one-year
life span, a company's brand catchphrase, like its flagship logo design, can
continue on for decades. "Heinz 57 Varieties" is still going strong after two
centuries have closed out, while dozens of Heinz Tomato Ketchup ad campaigns have come and gone over the past century.

In advertising, the slogan's role is to leave the primary brand message in
the minds of consumers. This usually is accomplished at the sign-off that ac-
companies or follows the advertiser's logo. It says, "If you get nothing else
from this TV spot, get this message!"

Now, here's a sobering fact: Most brand slogans don't even come close
to hitting a brand slam. A whopping 88 percent of them are ineffective because people don't have the slightest clue as to which brand slogan belongs
to what company or what industry is being referred to in that slogan. These
are the findings of my firm's testing of more than one hundred brand slogans with thousands of consumers since 1994.

To make my point, take this quick test. Identify the company behind each of these eight internationally advertised brand slogans. The answers are given at the end of this chapter.

a.   "Working to make a difference."
b.   "What you never thought possible."
c.   "We're there when you need us."
d.   "You've got a friend in the business."
e.   "The way the world works."
f.   "The power of partnership."
g.   "Do more."
h.   "We try harder."

OK, here are eleven brand slam brand slogans. Unless you've been living on another planet since the 1980s, you should know the company and the products behind each of these globally advertised brand catchphrases. Almost everyone in our test did.

"The Breakfast of Champions"
"Is that your final answer?"
"It's everywhere you want to be"
"The Ultimate Driving Machine"
"This Bud's for you"
"The Museum Watch"
"Good to the last drop"
"Plop, plop, fizz, fizz"
"We're bullish on America"
"It keeps going . . . and going"
"Don't leave home without it"

It doesn't take a rocket scientist to figure out what brand slogans are more effective communicators. The first seven could apply to almost any *Fortune* 1000 listed company. There are no word clues to help us identify the company, the products, or the industry. In the second group, we have word clues to help us visualize the company's product. Here's why each of these brand catchphrases stands out from the herd:

"The Breakfast of Champions" can only belong to one cereal—Wheaties.

When ABC's lawyers insisted that Regis Philbin, the TV host of the hit show *Who Wants to Be a Millionaire,* ask the contestants, "Is that your final answer?" the show's producers had no idea that these five words would become an identifiable tag line for the *Millionaire* show—but it did.

Visa's "It's everywhere you want to be" brand slogan capitalizes on this established brand's equity. Whether you're dining out with friends in Rome, purchasing an old carpet in Istanbul, renting a car in Sydney, or checking into a hotel in Copenhagen, the Visa credit card is accepted everywhere you are. That's a powerful brand message.

"The ultimate driving machine" brand slogan hit a nerve with yuppies in the 1970s and 1980s who had the financial means to own or lease a BMW car. Today, it's still the carmaker's tag line, denoting high quality standards in product design, engineering, and craftsmanship.

Anheuser-Busch's "This Bud's for you" brand slogan tells us exactly what the brand is and that we will be getting something special that only Budweiser, the No. 1 selling beer brand in America, can deliver.

"The Museum Watch": First, this brand slogan identifies the product. Second, how many watch brands are known to be "The Museum Watch"? Movado has to be the answer. When MoMA added the Movado wrist watch to its permanent design collection, the folks at Movado saw an opportunity for a memorable product catchphrase.

If you're a coffee aficionado, are there any five words more inviting than Maxwell House's "Good to the last drop" brand slogan? With more than 300 gourmet coffee brands in the marketplace, this tag line speaks for just one of them—Maxwell House.

It doesn't get any better than Alka-Seltzer's "plop, plop, fizz, fizz" brand theme line. It reminds people to put two large white tablets in a glass of water and wait to hear the fix before gulping down the concoction.

The word *bullish* instinctively brings to mind the NYSE and NASDAQ stock markets. And no one is more bullish on the financial markets than America's No. 1 brokerage firm—Merrill Lynch. Merrill Lynch's slogan "We're bullish on America," has kept its customers focused on long-term stock investments, and it encourages them to ignore occasional wild swings in the markets.

Energizer's pink bunny brand slogan "It keeps going . . . and going" has become a cultural icon of the ultimate message of longevity, perseverance, and determination. You'll see reference to this hare's famous advertising tag line in newspaper and magazine articles every month, and especially in reference to sports stars, politicians, and national heroes.

There's nothing like a warning to get consumers focused on your product. That was exactly the idea behind American Express' memorable brand slogan "Don't leave home without it." If you do, you might just be out of luck.

There's no doubt about it, great advertising catchphrases have put many company flagship brands on the world's map. What's more, once you do hit a brand slam "brand slogan," that line is unforgetable. Most frequent flyers couldn't tell you with certainty what colors and graphics are painted on the fuselage and tail of United Airlines planes. But ask them if they know what the airline's advertising brand slogan is and they'll tell you: "Fly the friendly skies of United."

Among dot-coms, much kudos go to Monster.com's "There's a better job out there" brand theme line. It's quite obvious from the word "job" that this is an online job search site.

Sun Microsystems, a worldwide provider of products, services, and support solutions for building and maintaining networking computing environments, scored a marketing coup with its brand slam brand slogan: "We're the dot com in .com." It positions Sun Microsystems as the undisputed leader among all dot-com companies, including Cisco Systems who pioneered the products that run the World Wide Web.

NEGATIVE WORDS CAN BACKFIRE

Brand catchphrases that have a negative word in them, like "not," "don't," or "doesn't," can sometimes create doubt in consumers' minds about a company's product and, in some cases, even a company's industry. GM Oldsmobile's 1988 advertising brand slogan "This is not your father's Oldsmobile" is a classic example of what not to do. Not only was it much-ridiculed by the advertising world, it actually distanced Oldsmobile from its glorious heyday of the 1950s and 1960s, when the automaker sold more cars than any other GM division. Many consumers and Oldsmobile diehards interpreted that brand message to be an apology by Olds for having manufactured and sold inferior cars to their parents.

I am not saying here to avoid at all cost a negative word in a brand slogan. Some of the most memorable brand slogans ever created have a negative word in them, like *"Don't* leave home without it," and "It melts in your mouth, *not* in your hand." A lot has to do with the verb that follows a "do not" warning. Here's an example.

An advertised brand catchphrase that says: *"Don't* trust your health care to anyone else," will only raise a "red flag" about the quality of health care service in America. Such a message could easily create unnecessary fear and anxiety for patients scheduled to undergo a surgical procedure. It also would raise questions about the integrity of the company behind such a baitlike slogan.

The word *no* often is confused by advertisers as being negative, when, in fact, it's really an effective word when you want to draw a comparison to competing products or services. The best example of this is Mercedes-Benz's famous brand slogan: "Engineered like *no* other car in the world."

But don't think for a moment that brand sloganeering is simply a matter of coming up with three or four catchy words. Devising a brand catchphrase that captures a company's mission, vision, or rallying cry can consume months of time or even a year or more. While many CEOs think they're up for the challenge, they would be well-advised to turn this task over to a proven brand sloganeer.

THE RIGHT BRAND SLOGAN IS LIKE WINNING THE LOTTO

Should the day ever come that General Mills decides to put its famed Wheaties cereal brand on the auction block, it's very likely that the winning bid will be in the billions of dollars. What makes the dollar valuation of this brand icon so high in my opinion goes beyond the product itself, the Wheaties brand name, the brand's logo, and the distinctive orange package design. What the buyer would be getting is one of the most unforgettable brand slogans ever invented for a consumer food product—"The Breakfast of Champions."

Now what added millions would you pay for a company whose brand slogan is "We're there when you need us?" As a brand specialist, I wouldn't advise my client to pay a dollar more than what the company is valued at without that brand slogan. Why? Because one of the first things the buyer will need to do is replace this advertising catchphrase with one that speaks only to this company's umbrella brand. Let's face it, this isn't the only company in America that's there when you need them. But how many TV game shows can say, "Is that your final answer?"

LESSONS LEARNED

1. The more the slogan resonates with a big advertising idea, the more memorable it will become in the minds of consumers.

2. The best brand slogans consist of three, four, or five words that speak to the essence, uniqueness, or spirit of a company's flagship brand head-on. Slogans that exceed five words are too difficult for most people to remember.

3. At a minimum, your brand's slogan should help consumers narrow it down to a few brands, including yours, that could possibly fit that slogan's profile or description. If it doesn't, you might as well say at the close of your print ad or TV spot, "Our brand's tag line is dedicated to every company out there."

4. If you want consumers to remember the brand that's behind your brand's catchphrase, simply mention the name. "The difference is Merrill Lynch" and "Ford, built to last" are two good examples.

5. Keep the message positive, and if you do use the negative word *don't,* pay close attention to the verb that follows it.

Here are the answers to the test from earlier in the chapter. Don't feel badly if you missed any of them. It's not your fault the company failed to deliver their message to you.

a. Phillip Morris

b. Motorola

c. Ryder Trucks

d. Gateway Computers

e. FedEx

f. Zurich-American Insurance Group

g. American Express

h. Avis

9

BRAND SLAM
PACKAGE DESIGN

"Lead, follow, or get the hell out of the way."
U.S. Four Star General George Patton

BREAKFAST OF CHAMPIONS

When I look back on the great package designs of the twentieth century, one stands out in my mind and probably in the minds of millions of other people. I'm talking about Wheaties—the popular cereal in the orange box that was born in 1924. As the story goes, a Minneapolis man accidentally spilled a wheat bran mixture on a hot stove and when he tasted the crispy flakes, he knew he had hit on something really big. He passed on his find to the people at Washburn Crosby Company, forerunner of General Mills, and in 1924, Washburn's Gold Medal Wheat Flakes made its debut. A year later, the product's name was shortened to Wheaties, which happens to be one of the great "invented" consumer product brand names of all time.

In 1926, "Have you tried Wheaties?" was America's first singing commercial, and it put the brand Wheaties on the nation's map. But the big brand slam came in 1933, when the Wheaties brand became associated with sports. Wheaties became "The Breakfast of Champions." And those four words have become one of America's most memorable brand slogans.

One of the great athletes to appear on the cereal's box face, endorsing Wheaties as "The Breakfast of champions," was Babe Ruth. The next brand slam came when Wheaties sponsored the first televised sports broadcast in 1939. Gold Medal pole-vaulting champion Bob Richards directed the

Wheaties Sports Federation and served as the brand's TV spokesperson from 1956 to 1970. Bruce Jenner, Decathlon Gold Medalist in track and field who also appeared on the Wheaties box, took over the role of spokesperson in 1977. He promoted the brand as nutritional food that goes hand-in-hand with physical fitness.

In the 1980s, Gold Medalist Mary Lou Retton became the first female spokesperson when her face appeared on the front of the orange box. Walter Payton, Chris Evert, and Michael Jordan all appeared on the Wheaties box promoting the cereal's great taste and health benefits.

A decade later, Tiger Woods appeared on box. Woods is now ranked the No. 1 golfer in the world and considered by many sports writers to be the greatest golfer that's ever lived. Now that's hitting a brand slam.

In 1999, Wheaties celebrated its seventy-fifth anniversary by re-releasing the original packages of ten great Wheaties champions as selected by American consumers through a "Vote for Your Favorite Wheaties Champion" Web site promotion. The favorite champions of all-time are Babe Ruth, Lou Gehrig, Jackie Robinson, Cal Ripken, Jr., Mary Lou Retton, John Elway, the 1980 U.S. Olympic Hockey Team, Walter Payton, Michael Jordan, and Tiger Woods. To build on its many brand slam boxes, Wheaties is releasing a commemorative package series honoring each of these ten champions.

Another brand marketing coup was honoring the World Champion New York Yankees, who won their 25th World Championship by defeating the Atlanta Braves and sweeping the 1999 World Series, on a special limited-edition Wheaties box. The box's front panel featured the Yankees' inspirational leader and manager, Joe Torre. "Wheaties' heritage is closely tied to baseball, so we think it's very fitting to honor one of baseball's most storied franchises as we close out this century," said Wheaties marketing manager, Jim Murphy.

Seventy-five champions have graced the fabled orange box beginning with the Yankees' Lou Gehrig.[1] If there's a sports celebrity on a box of cereal, it has to be Wheaties.

THE LITTLE BLUE BOX WITH THE WHITE RIBBON

She may be your sweet sixteen, your bride to be, your wife of ten years, your mother, or your grandmother, but take out of your jacket pocket a little blue box tied with a white ribbon and I can assure you that you're going to see a big smile on that person's face. The little blue box tied with a white ribbon has become an instant identifiable Tiffany & Company brand icon even if you don't see the discreet Tiffany logo on the box lid. Now that's WOW.

---

1. *Source: Wheaties.com.*

Regardless of what gift is inside that little blue box, or what it cost, it says to the recipient of the gift that she or he is worth Tiffany. "Keep it simple" or "make it look simple" is one of the time-tested secrets to building a powerhouse brand. In the case of Tiffany & Company, the packaging of any store item is all about simplicity and good taste.

A Spoon for Your Yogurt

Everyday, millions of people in America's workforce are just too busy to have a sit-down lunch at a restaurant. So, they head straight to a supermarket or convenience store to pick up a snack to satisfy their appetite and give them the fuel they need to finish the day.

What better health snack is there than an 8-ounce Colombo Classic—a fruit-on-the-bottom yogurt that you stir to blend? All flavors including Key Lime Pie, Lemon Meringue, Strawberry Colada, and Raspberry Lemonade in the Colombo Light line have 0 grams of fat and only 100 calories. Can you imagine watching someone on a park bench eating yogurt out of a container with their tongue. It's not a pretty sight; obviously, consumption of a yogurt snack requires a spoon. But suppose you stop somewhere for a Colombo yogurt and they don't have any plastic spoons or you forget to pick one up.

Hey, I've got an idea! What about creating a snap-out spoon in a plastic container lid of a ready-to-eat Colombo yogurt snack? Colombo did just that with its new "Spoon in Lid!" yogurt line in 1999, and it hit a brand slam with yogurt lovers across America.

An Easy Way to Test Batteries

Invention and innovation have become the hallmarks of the Energizer battery brand. Founded more than 100 years ago, the company (Eveready) has played an important role in how people play, work, and communicate. It has a history of firsts. In 1896, Eveready was the first commercial manufacturer in America to develop dry cell batteries. In the late 1950s, Energizer was the first to introduce alkaline technology, which revolutionized portable power. The new alkaline batteries opened doors for new portable consumer products. In 1989, Energizer introduced the world's first AA size lithium battery and became the only company to sell this type of battery. In 1995, Energizer was first to introduce an on-battery tester that allowed consumers to check the power left in their alkaline batteries. In 1997, Energizer launched a high performance long-lasting AA battery for power-draining products including digital cameras and cell phones.

But hands down, it's the Energizer battery equipped with a gauge-style tester for an accurate read on remaining power that hit a brand slam for millions of consumers. All you need to do is press two green spots firmly and the word *Good* appears in the tester window at full power. If the color black remains in the window, it means there's only 25 percent power remaining.

LESSONS LEARNED

1. It takes big ideas to create packaging design WOW, not strategies, strategies, and more strategies.

2. There's nothing like a great package design to sell a me-too or generic product.

3. Don't mess with a package design that consumers find irresistible unless what you're changing to is packed with more WOW.

4. Look for innovative ways to make your product's packaging more useful to consumers.

5. A distinctive package color can set your product apart from the herd.

10

PR: WHAT WORKS AND WHAT DOESN'T

Every workday in America news reporters, journalists, assignment editors, TV anchors and producers receive bundles of PR press kits and news releases announcing a new product introduction, merger, new corporate CEO appointment, or other business news event. When the same media people go online to read their email, their box is full with PR-related announcements. When they check their fax machine, dozens of news releases are piled up in the machine's paper holder. When they check voice mail, it's filled with messages mostly left by PR people vying for a chance to pitch their client's news story to them. Then there are all those hand-delivered engraved invitations to a press luncheon at the Waldorf Astoria, a cocktail party at New York's Plaza Hotel, or a black-tie dinner event on a chartered yacht—all of which are designed to win over these media people or get them to cover a corporate or brand news event.

But the bulk of this daily communication avalanche never gets read or listened to by the recipients. It's tossed into waste bins, deleted from email, or calls are not returned. Of those PR pitches that do make it to an editorial review, maybe two or three receive a green light for print publication or TV. This is the reality of the public relations business. To earn big fees in this field, a firm has to have a track record for getting its clients' stories aired on prime time and cable news networks, and on the front pages of the nation's most read business newspapers and magazines. Of course, if a PR firm puts out on the news wire that MCI Worldcom purchased Sprint for a whopping $129 billion, making it the largest amount ever paid for a company at the time of the announcement, it's certain to garner nonstop worldwide news coverage. But to test the mettle of your company's PR staff or your PR agency, ask it to get around-the-clock TV and print media coverage for a change in a product description or product labeling that amounts to nothing more than "so what else is new?"

CRAYOLA REWRITES HISTORY WITH A BRAND SLAM

It's simply amazing: Binney & Smith, maker of Crayola crayons, announced to the media that one of its colored crayons found in Crayola 48-, 64-, and 90-count box assortments sold nationwide would no longer be called "indian red," but "chestnut." Guess what happened? The event was covered by ABC, NBC, and CBS morning, evening, and late-evening news programs, as well as CNN, CNNfn, and CNBC cable news networks. Hey folks, we're only talking about a single crayon color name change here, not something that's going to have an impact on our daily lives. Yet the announcement of the renaming of one crayon garnered huge media attention, while more important business and national events happening on that same day were not mentioned by these news programs.

How Binney & Smith's PR people pulled off this brand slam coup offers valuable insight to every manufacturer of an established flagship consumer brand. For starters, they made the event appear to the media that "history was being rewritten." The decision to change the color of the reddish-brown crayon formerly known as indian red to chestnut has officially taken its place alongside of "prussian blue" and "flesh" as one of only three crayons in Crayola's history to ever be renamed. One would have thought the Vatican had announced that the Gospel of Saint Mark in the Catholic-version of the New Testament was being rewritten.

The announcement was obviously aimed at recalling memories of a time when we were kids drawing pictures with Crayola crayons at home or in kindergarten. "The history of your childhood playtime and your children's future memories of drawing with Crayola crayons have been forever changed" was the message that Binney & Smith's PR people pitched to the nation's media, and they took it hook, line, and sinker.

Binney & Smith also made the crayon's new color name a contest with consumers. After considering more than 250,000 name suggestions from nearly 100,000 crayon enthusiasts of all ages, the color name chestnut was chosen. That's like commissioning a study to identify the color of a ripened banana peel and, after one year of exhaustive consumer research, zeroing in on the word *yellow.* But it doesn't stop there. Each of the 155 respondents who suggested chestnut earned a place in Crayola color history; they all received a "Certificate of Crayola Crayon Authorship" and an assortment of the company's products. To pique further media interest, Crayola released the names of the runners up—auburn, autumn red, barn red, and mahogany.

There are hundreds of products in the marketplace with a rich brand heritage. Reminding the media of a brand's history and the role that it has played in our childhood days can win over even the most hard-core editors.

CAMPBELL'S SOUP DROWNS IMAGE IN NEW LABEL DESIGN

I recall as a youngster coming home from school on a cold winter's day and heading straight to the kitchen in search of my mother. "Mom, is there anything to eat?" I would ask.

"I'll make you a hot bowl of Campbell's soup," was often her answer. The prepared soup sprinkled with crumbled Ritz crackers floating on top really hit the spot. I am sure that as a kid, you too can recount similar experiences with Campbell's condensed soups.

But what stands out most in my mind about Campbell's were those standout red-and-white condensed soup labels that the late artist Andy Warhol raised to a brand icon status with his now famous silk-screen art of the cans. Although simplistic in design, those red-and-white labels were instantly recognizable as Campbell's line of condensed soups no matter where you were shopping.

So when your product line's label design appears in art museums around the world, is undisputedly recognized as one of America's great brand icons, and is cherished by millions of moms and kids, why change it? Well, Campbell's Soup Company did just that; its new soup label debuted August 26, 1999. The new label story was picked up by national TV news programs including cable news networks. But did the new design, featuring the addition of a bowl of soup on the label's face and other graphic changes, hit a brand slam or even a home run with consumers and the media? Based on the consensus of 100-plus homemakers that my firm polled after the new label aired on TV, it was at best an infield hit. Many felt that the original label had more going for it than its new replacement. How then could Campbell's, with so much brand marketing muscle and consumer research experience, not have hit a PR brand slam with the folks that we talked to? Here are my thoughts on the reasons why.

When a company's flagship consumer brand and its product-line label achieve global recognition or icon status, the management of those assets requires the utmost care and judicial marketing prudence. True, many famous food brand labels do undergo periodic refinements in graphics, color, or even a new product tag line to keep them current with the times. Betty Crocker, Aunt Jemima, Uncle Ben's, and the Quaker Oat's Man have all undergone several facelifts, hairdos, and wardrobe changes since the end of World War II. But in almost every case, consumers were unaware of these cosmetic changes at the time they were made. In short, these marketers pay close attention to preserving the brand's historical visual identity on the packaging label.

In the case of Campbell's, its simple red-and-white label said condensed soups loud and clear to consumers without the need of a product illustration. More important, it confirmed the brand's heritage and the wholesomeness of the product to people of all ages. The big gamble here was that the new label implied: "This is not the original Campbell's condensed soup that mom prepared and served to you when you were a youngster, but a new soup line extension." Remember what happened in the 1980s when Coca-Cola announced the launch of "New Coke"? Coke enthusiasts revolted and it wasn't long before the No. 1 maker of soft drinks announced the arrival of Coca-Cola Classic with a 100 percent guarantee to Coke lovers worldwide that it was "The Real Thing."

The idea behind labeling any consumer product is to establish an instant recognizable brand identity—an identity that assures consumers they are buying the same product that they had experienced before. Take Lea & Perrins' "The Original Worcestershire Sauce" since 1835. The light-brown paper label wrapped over a slender dark-brown glass bottle with a dark-brown screw-off cap tells us we're buying the original Worcestershire Sauce that makes any meal and a "Bloody Mary" more memorable. Likewise, the diamond-shaped white label mounted on a slender round-shouldered bottle with a tall neck and bright-red screw-off cap immediately tells us it's the world-renowned "Tabasco Brand" pepper sauce produced by McIlhenny Company. To radically change these and other brand label icons would be an act of marketing insanity, to put it mildly.

Here's the most important question that any marketer should ask before radically changing a consumer label with an iconic brand status: "Is it to-die-for?" By that I mean, is the new label so compelling to the eye that it receives a standing ovation from consumers and the media? If you can't answer in the affirmative, then think twice about making any radical changes or you could face a costly failure. In the case of Campbell's Soup, its new soup label doesn't say WOW, which is a must when you're out to hit a brand slam. Further, it opened the door for other national brands including Progresso to introduce a similar-looking soup can label design. That could never have happened if the original red-and-white Campbell's classic soup label remained as it was.

On May 18, 2000, Campbell's Soup Company once again announced that it was redesigning its canned soup labels. For the previous three quarters, the company's profits had been on a decline.

Lessons Learned

1. Never put out a PR news story to the press stating or even inferring that your company has relaxed the product standards of its flagship brand. It will surely diminish the image of the brand's

name and the product as held in the minds of consumers, investors, employees, suppliers, media people, and everyone else.

2. If you're going to announce a change in the standards of a recognized brand, or a change in the spokesperson who has become synonymous with your brand over the years, make sure the change is a noticeable improvement. Otherwise, you run the risk of a consumer backlash. And, should you suddenly need to retract your words, you may find yourself with a PR disaster, which could prove to be costly, not to mention embarrassing.

3. Never underestimate the emotional loyalty that consumers have to your company's umbrella brand or one of your flagship brands.

WHEN RELIGION ENTERS THE PICTURE

The last thing that most corporate CEOs want to experience on their watch is a public furor or controversy over a new product or their management of an established consumer brand-name product. Ironically, however, in the PR field, history has shown that a public outcry or controversy over the content of an intellectual work, or the people or organizations identified with the project, often results in blockbuster sales for the product or event. Bring religion into the picture, and it's almost a sure bet that the news media and tabloids will be covering the story for weeks, if not months. All of that translates into millions of free dollars of publicity for the event or product, and a brand slam coup for the PR architects who fueled the media's interest. While I can mention dozens of examples in the past century, the following incidents stand out most in my mind.

The rock opera *Jesus Christ Superstar* was released in October 1970 amid much controversy. Written by Andrew Lloyd Webber and Tim Rice, the musical centers around the last seven days of Christ's life as seen through the eyes of Judas. Christian organizations in America yelled "foul ball" for what they saw to be irreverent behavior. For instance, the play implies a relationship between Mary Magdalene and Jesus. Others criticized the rock opera for what they interpreted was a depiction of Christ as a homosexual who surrounded himself with prostitutes. The criticisms went beyond words—an Argentine theater that was staging the performance was burnt to the ground. The media coverage of the outcries to boycott *Superstar* only increased the lines of people waiting to buy tickets to the performance in London and then in New York. Today, *Jesus Christ Superstar* is a monument in musical history. Many acclaimed musicals rise and fall and are replaced. This one is still being staged in a U.S. tour thirty years later. In late March 2000, an updated version of Webber and Rice's hit musical opened again on Broadway.

Here's another example of the PR power of religion. The 1996 concert tour of the rock band KISS was labeled "satanic" by church leaders and evangelists. Their heeded warnings to parents to keep their teenage girls and boys away from the rock concert only fueled the desires of young teens to attend the event at any cost. The PR promoters couldn't have been more happy with the ensuing media's attention. The KISS concert tour was sold out nationwide.

Likewise, Salman Rushdie's fictional book, *The Satanic Verses* (published in February 1989 by Penguin USA), created quite a stir. In Betsy Hearne's review in *The Economist,* she notes that Rushdie's book takes its title from an incident in Muhammad's life when the people of Mecca persuaded the prophet to add two verses to the Koran to give angelic status to three of their popular goddesses. The reviewer goes on to note that Muhammad later removed the verses believing that they were inspired by Satan himself. Gibreel and Saladin, the two main characters in Rushdie's book, stand for good and evil, angel and devil. Muhammad enters in the book's central story. The reader is suddenly transported to Jahila, "city of sand," where the prophet Mahound replays the old story of Muhammad as he receives his divine revelation of good in evil and evil in good. The story ends simply and with considerable power.

Rushdie's book outraged Islamic fundamentalists around the world—perhaps because the prophet Muhammad was a character in the author's comic plot. Whatever the reason, on February 14, 1989, the Ayatollah Khomeini, Iran's leader at that time, called for the author's immediate death. The national attention given to the Ayatollah's reported $1 million bounty on Rushdie's head, and to the whereabouts of the author who went into hiding, provided the fuel needed to rocket the book to the top of the *New York Times* bestseller list. For Penguin, the Ayatollah's death sentence handed it the script for a PR brand slam coup; the publisher's PR people ran with it.

A similar high-profile event occurred in New York City in 1999. As the millennium neared its close, New York Mayor Rudolph Giuliani threatened to evict the Brooklyn Museum and cut off all city subsidies over the "Sensation" exhibit, which he called "offensive art." The threat became a news story that reached far across the country. As in the case of Iran's Ayatollah Khomeini, Giuliani's furor over the art exhibit could not have been more helpful to set the stage for an international PR brand slam for a public, subsidized museum that previously was overshadowed by New York's iconic brand-name art museums MoMA, the Metropolitan Museum of Art, and the Guggenheim Museum.

Many New Yorkers shared the opinion of *New York Times* art critic Michael Kimmelman who stated, "This time Mayor Rudolph Giuliani is playing the role of a stern dad to a group of British artists whom he seems to regard as naughty teenagers."[1]

---

1. New York Times, *September 24, 1999.*

The exhibition consisted of works belonging to Charles Saatchi, a principal of the London-based advertising agency Saatchi & Saatchi and a noted art collector. Among the bizarre works were a dead shark floating in a tank, part of a dead sheep in a closed container being eaten by live maggots, and a collage of the Virgin Mary with cutouts from pornographic magazines and several clumps of elephant dung attached to the work. The mayor and other public interest groups were in an uproar. But, as Kimmelman noted in his piece, "We have young artists doing what young artists always do to get attention."

After the dust settled, attendance to the three-month art exhibit set a record for the Brooklyn Museum. On the final day of the exhibit, I took a late lunch at Bice, my favorite New York Italian restaurant. "I went to Brooklyn today to see the 'Sensation' exhibit before it closed," said my waiter, Nick. "I felt it was a once-in-a-life-time experience happening in New York that you had to see." Nick's words said it all about this PR brand slam that will be talked about for years to come.

On March 27, 2000, the New York City Mayor's office announced that a settlement was reached with the Brooklyn Museum and the issue was now closed. The museum will continue to receive subsidies from the city. It was a clear victory for art and for the museum itself.

HARRY POTTER MANIA

Booksellers across the nation say it's the most phenomenal book release ever in the history of book publishing. Unless you were out of touch with the nation's news during the week of July 3 to July 10, 2000, you must have heard about J.K. Rowling's book *Harry Potter and the Goblet of Fire*. This was the author's fourth book in the wildly popular series about the exploits of Harry Potter, the boy wizard. Not since *Gone with the Wind* has a best-selling book swept the nation like Harry Potter, reported *New York Times* book-review critic David D. Kirkpatrick.[2]

The two-week long publicity that Rowling's book received by the media in America and the United Kingdom was not by accident. Scholastic, the publisher of Harry Potter books in America, formed an alliance with Amazon.com to market advance orders of the book. It was history in the making on the Internet with the number of pre-orders updated hourly on Amazon.com's Web site. By July 8, 2000, the book's release date, 370,000 book orders had been placed online with Amazon.com. Then Amazon.com formed an unprecedented alliance with FedEx to deliver 300,000 preordered books faster than an owl messenger on the release

2. *"Harry Potter Magic Halts Bedtime for Youngsters"* by D.D. Kirkpatrick (New York Times, July 9, 2000).

date. Get this, FedEx had 9,000 workers delivering those books on Saturday, July 8, 2000. According to the *New York Times,* Barnes & Noble retail stores and its online store site received 360,000 preorders of the book, more than ten times as many as any previous title. The stores sold 114,000 more books the first hour after the book's release.

Scholastic announced that it produced 3.8 million books in the first printing of the fourth Harry Potter sequel. This news was picked up by morning and evening TV news programs. To add to the drama, Scholastic enforced strict secrecy about the fourth book's contents and required booksellers to keep all copies under wraps until 12:01 A.M., Saturday, July 8, 2000. Amazon.com hired additional security personnel at its distribution centers to ensure that no book would fall into the hands of an employee prior to the official release time; that in itself made for more TV news coverage.

While people were waiting to get the fourth Harry Potter book on a special FedEx upgrade offer, Amazon.com was reminding its millions of site visitors to buy the first three hardcover Harry Potter books to get up to speed for reading the fourth book in the series. It also created four splendid and unique Harry Potter e-Cards to announce the book's coming arrival by FedEx to be used by those who preordered the book for a friend or family member.

Big bookstore chains like Barnes & Noble and rival mom-and-pop local bookstores across the country got into the act by throwing Harry Potter parties at the magical 12:01 A.M. book-release hour. Many of the bookstores opened their doors at midnight to a line of hundreds of children and parents awaiting their first chance to buy *Harry Potter and the Goblet of Fire.* Witches performed stunts and distributed wizard-made snacks and drinks to the kids. Some bookstores hired magicians to perform and asked their employees to dress up in wizard costumes.

The first three books in the series already sold more than 18 million copies in the United States. "For the moment, the hottest trend at elementary schools and summer camps is not a video game or a movie—it is an old-fashioned, ink-and-paper book, said *New York Times* reporter Kirkpatrick.

Talk about a PR coup. Five years ago, J.K. Rowling was living in England on welfare. Today, she's making millions on book royalties. But there are millions yet to roll in for her when Time Warner, who is the official licensee for Harry Potter merchandise, rolls out in 2001, a mind-boggling array of children's products branded with Harry Potter and the other characters created by Rowling. We're talking maybe a billion dollars or more in worldwide merchandising sales. And the word is out that the first Harry Potter movie is in the works.

Barbara Marcus, president of Scholastic children's books pulled off an amazing PR brand slam. She brought together alliances of big-league brand names like Amazon.com and FedEx to market Harry Potter. She stressed to the nation's media that an historic event in book publishing was in the making, "Nothing like it has ever been done before" was Scholastic's PR theme. While she kept most of the book's content a secret, she leaked out a few tidbits of information to the press: Will Harry fall in love? Who's the character that dies? Is Hogwarts safe from danger? "Hey kids, don't you want to find out?" was the bait. She made sure that the book's jacket cover was shown on all of the TV news programs to add to the excitement and consumer demand. The jacket's illustration of Harry Potter, now fourteen-years-old in this fantasy series, correctly positioned the fourth book to target readers aged 9 through 12.

One TV coanchor asked: "Why are people going crazy to pre-order a book that will be in bookstores three days from now?" Answer: That's the power behind a PR brand slam!

LESSONS LEARNED

1. Emphasize that your brand's history is being rewritten.
2. Build up enthusiasm for your brand's heritage, integrity, and values.
3. Highlight the fact that childhood memories of your brand will last a lifetime.
4. Urge involvement or feedback with enthusiasts of your brand before releasing a news story to the press.
5. Strive for a news headline that has WOW impact.

11

MEGABRAND MERGERS
HIT A BRAND SLAM

Want to hit a brand slam this year? Outshine the competition? It's simple—just merge with a company that has a premier brand name recognized throughout the world.

Imagine Disney merging with the Vatican. The smallest country in the world, governed by the Holy See, would be transformed into a 102-acre world-class "Disney Theme Park" with Saint Peter's cathedral as the park's crown jewel. Sound far-fetched? Maybe, but long before there were masters of the twentieth-century brand universe like Walt Disney, there was Pope Julius II. Donald Trump, who is known for demolishing an entire city block to erect one of his signature buildings, is no match for the pope who gave the order in 1505 to demolish Saint Peter's church in Rome. I am talking about the church that the Roman emperor Constantine commissioned to be built in the fourth century and which was considered to be the most holy place in all of Europe during the Renaissance period.

Most megabrand mergers aren't quite that dramatic. But two major airlines grabbed the media spotlight when on May 25, 2000, U.S. Airways' board of directors announced it had approved the acquisition of the company by United Airlines' parent, UAL. The merger represents nearly a $12 billion buyout deal by UAL, giving United Airlines a network of routes and airport hubs to eastern coastal cities that it did not have before.

The announcement and what the deal meant to shareholders of both companies and consumers were the topics of discussion by the anchors of TV broadcasting and cable news networks for two days running. In addition, the merger story made front-page newspaper headlines. It would cost about $100 million to buy comparable air time through TV commercials. Now that's a brand slam in anyone's book.

However, the big "earthquake" in the advertising and public relations communities took place on May 12, 2000, when WPP Group announced a $4.7 billion acquisition of Young & Rubicam to create the world's leading marketing communications services company. It was the highest amount ever paid for an advertising agency network. With Y&R in its stable, the WPP Group became the industry leader, offering its expanded client base, which includes the majority of the Fortune Global 500 and the Nasdaq 100, a comprehensive array of resources in all service categories. On a pro forma basis, the combined group had revenues of $5.2 billion for the year ending December 31, 1999.

The transaction brought together stellar brands from major marketing disciplines. These included global advertising giants Ogilvy & Mather, J. Walter Thompson, and Y&R advertising; in addition to four of the world's largest public relations firms, Hill and Knowlton, Burson-Marsteller, Ogilvy Public Relations Worldwide, and Cohn and Wolfe; as well as Impiric and Ogilvy One, the industry leaders in direct and interactive marketing.

Both WPP and Y&R have built leading-edge capabilities to assist their clients in e-business and interactive marketing. The combined group now has the broadest Internet portfolio in the industry, capturing dot-com ad spending and providing the industry's leading digital services.

The deal was a major coup for WPP Group and its founder and CEO, Sir Martin Sorrell, who basked for several days in the media limelight after his stunning capture of the premier agency brand Y&R. Just thirty years ago, the giants of industry would have fired their advertising or PR agency if there was even the slightest appearance of a conflict of interest with a major competitor. Sorrell has done a remarkable job of persuading WPP's clients that having a full spectrum of services to meet their every communications need in all global major markets will create significant growth and value for them. Plus his repeated assurances in person to WPP clients that its advertising and public relations agencies operate independently of each other went a long way to calm jittery nerves. In that sense, one could say Sorrell hit a diplomatic home run with WPP's clients. But for WPP's shareholders and employees, Sir Martin hit a brand slam by conquering the world's largest advertising market—America.

Sorrell's rise from a financial genius at Saatchi & Saatchi in 1986, to industry visionary is a colorful and controversial story. His original business plan for WPP Group was not acquisitions of ad agencies. Then his eye caught the sight of a big-name ad agency in America that was underperforming financially—so much for his business plan. In 1987, in a $556 million hostile takeover, WPP acquired J. Walter Thompson Co. To help pay for the acquisition, Sorrell sold a Tokyo office building for $100 million that was owned by the acquiring agency.

Sir Martin's next hostile takeover of Ogilvy & Mather Worldwide for $864 million in 1989, prompted much industry criticism of this Brit who was relatively unknown in the United States. The deal so outraged O&M's former chairman David Ogilvy, that he publicly called Sorrell an "odious little shit," which of course made front-page news. To end the controversy and win over David Ogilvy, Sorrell put him on the payroll as honorary chairman and assured O&M's clients that it would be David Ogilvy, not him, that would have the final say on the agency's creative direction. It turned out to be a smart tactical move for Sorrell.[1]

In the automotive world, Chrysler and Daimler-Benz set an all-time record for the biggest industrial merger ever in early May 1998. The story about the new Daimler Chrysler umbrella brand name received nonstop worldwide TV and newspaper coverage for almost five consecutive days. Chrysler and Mercedes-Benz brand logos appeared together on the covers of leading business magazines, which had to make Chrysler's long-time U.S. rivals Ford and GM blink not once, but several times. Going to the altar with the world's premier carmaker was nothing short of a brand slam merger coup for Chrysler's shareholders, dealers, and employees.

But nothing tops America Online's (AOL) announced plans to acquire Time Warner on January 10, 2000, for stock and debt. The deal initially worth a whopping $166 billion dropped $21 billion in value the next day as investors grew more critical of the mammoth corporate merger, worried that high-flying AOL could become bogged down by the job of integrating the slower-growing Time Warner.[2]

Here was AOL, an Internet start-up that nobody knew in the mid-1990s, going for Time, which owns and publishes thirty-two magazines including *Time, Sports Illustrated, People, Fortune,* and *Entertainment Weekly.* Time also houses Warner Music Group, which includes Warner Brothers, Atlantic, and Elektra Records; Warner Brothers studios; and is part-owner of the WB television network. In addition, Time Warner is the largest owner of cable systems in America including CNN, HBO, and Cinemax cable networks.

As the Fox Market Wire news brief pointed out, AOL needs Time Warner's 13 million cable-TV lines to deliver the next generation of Internet technology to consumers—high speed access that is up to 100 times faster than through conventional telephone lines. At the same time, Time Warner gets access to AOL's customers to market its movies, magazines, and television shows over the Internet.[3]

Such megabrand mergers have catapulted the combined companies' flagship brands to global news attention overnight.

---

1. *The Knight That Would Be King"* by Laurel Wentz (Advertising Age, *May 15, 2000)*
2. Fox News Online, *January 11, 2000.*
3. *"Time Warner, AOL stock plunge as investors reconsider merger deal"* (Fox Market Wire, *January 11, 2000).*

LESSONS LEARNED

1. Merge only with a premium brand in your industry that will make your company the industry leader.

2. Look for an organization that's compatible with yours and one that shares a common philosophy and culture with your customers and employees.

3. A good merger partner will expand your company's geographical reach and will bring the people and assets needed to create significant growth and value for your shareholders.

4. Join forces with a company that can accelerate your vision for the future.

5. To move forward, you need a competitive advantage that takes you to the next level. The right merge partner will do that.

6. Above all, buy a company with talented people who are eager to stay on after the merger is finalized and are committed to building a first-class organization.

12

A BRAND SLAM MARRIAGE OF POWERHOUSE BRANDS

Had you proposed to an industry giant back in the early 1970s that it pay the cost to produce and air commercials that tie in with another company's brand-name product or service, you would have been fired on the spot or run out of town.

The world of brand marketing has changed dramatically. If your company is not forming marriages with other companies' powerhouse brands, you're at a distinct disadvantage in today's marketplace. I'm not talking about mergers here; I'm talking about linking your company's flagship brands with other companies' flagship brands or celebrities in advertising, sales promotion, and public relations to hit a brand slam with consumers.

BRAND MARRIAGES THAT WORKED

Breyers Ice Cream Blends in Big-Name Snack Brands

It's just ice cream, right? Not anymore. Now you can get Breyers ice cream with chunks of Nabisco's Oreo cookies blended into the product. If that doesn't make your mouth water, there's Breyers ice cream with chunks of Reese's Milk Chocolate Peanut Butter Cups packed into the product. Now that's WOW.

Red Lobster Relies on FedEx to Deliver Freshness

The very name of this restaurant chain says that lobster is its house specialty. Of course, if all Red Lobsters were located along the New England coastline, you obviously wouldn't need to advertise that you have fresh lobsters. But when your restaurants dot America's landscape, that's another story. To assure us that fresh lobsters are delivered each day to its restaurants, we see FedEx planes taking off and landing in Red Lobster's TV commercials.

Infiniti Promotes Bose Audio Sound System

On its Web site (infiniti.com), Infiniti makes this point: "Sometimes the difference between those who insist on quality, and those who insist on the indisputable best, is obvious." It then goes on to say that Infiniti cars come equipped with a Bose audio sound system designed specifically for the car's interior. From Infiniti's standpoint, it's a plus to have the Bose name appear on the face of the sound system mounted in the car's dashboard.

Uncle Ben's Ties a Knot with Tyson Chicken

Uncle Ben's new Rice Bowls are the answer to today's hectic lifestyles. Just seven minutes to heat up in a microwave and you've got a meal to satisfy your taste buds with no clean up. There are six Rice Bowls with chicken: Sweet & Sour Chicken, Chicken Bombay, Honey Dijon Chicken, Chicken & Vegetable, Szechuan Chicken, and Teriyaki Chicken. To create more WOW appeal for the frozen meal, Uncle Ben's touts that it's quality Tyson chicken in every bowl. The people who came up with the Rice Bowls concept, the brand's name, the package design, and the advertising spots have collectively hit one massive brand slam. More important, Uncle Ben's is once again a hot brand in supermarkets thanks to the Rice Bowls concept.

Amazon.com Links Up with Sotheby's Auctioneer House

Talk about marketing coups, Amazon.com pulled off a big one when it formed a brand marriage with Sotheby's. Visit Amazon.com's site and you're just a click away from the first step to selling or buying a collectable item online with the world's premier auctioneer.

American Express Is No Stranger to Brand Marriages

It's safe to say that American Express' Card Divisions helped pioneer the concept of forming marriages with other company brands. It's newest brand partnership is with SFX, the No. 1 concert presenter and promoter of the hottest music shows.

b'jan

beverly hills | designer for men

Bijan's distinctive handwritten logo reminds an international clientele that this master designer has his hand in everything he creates and markets under the Bijan brand.

Embracing life's twists and turns, Bijan launched bijan with a twist fragrance in Spring 2001. A single intricately converging spiral made of brass and immersed in 14K gold encompasses the bottle with a sense of infinite mobility.

Bijan, CEO and creative head of the Bijan menswear collection and Bijan fragrance empire.

The $10 million newly renovated House of Bijan on Rodeo Drive, Beverly Hills. The entrance of the boutique features a breathtaking two-story high glass and mahogany door.

Interior of the House of Bijan . . . an amber-colored crystal chandelier filled with over 1,000 authentic Bijan perfume bottles hangs above the grand staircase leading up to the designer's private menswear collection.

More than any typographical logo rendering could, David Ogilvy's handwritten name offers value beyond the graphics. It is bold, elegant, evocative, human, timeless, and uniquely the visual brand for this world-class advertising agency.

Inside the grand street-level lobby of Ogilvy & Mather's worldwide headquarters in New York, you can't miss the gigantic black and white photo of a contemplative-looking David Ogilvy, the agency's founder, in his signature striped shirt and suspenders. Prior to his passing in 1999, Ogilvy was hailed by his peers as being the greatest ad man of the twentieth century.

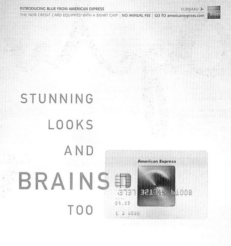

Ogilvy's recent brand slam print ad campaigns include "Dream with Your Eyes Wide Open" (The ad theme line reminds young girls of the most prized play doll in the world–Barbie.), "The Greatest Risk Is Not Taking One" (ad campaign underscores AIG's businesses–insurance and financial services), and "Stunning Looks and Brains Too" (ad campaign helps us to remember that the new American Express Blue Card has a built-in chip for added fraud protection).

⊙HermanMiller

The Herman Miller logo design is just as contemporary today as it was in the 1950s when it made its debut.

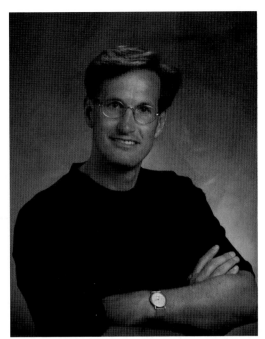

Herman Miller's CEO, Mike Volkema, presides over a collection of home and office seating, furniture, and open office systems that is sought after the world over.

It's in the movies, on TV, in magazine ads, in museum design collections, and working hard in offices everywhere. Winner of countless awards, including BusinessWeek Design of the Decade, it was a breakthrough when introduced in 1994. You can't miss its one-of-a-kind look. And when you sit down, you'll feel what all the fuss is about—Herman Miller's Aeron chair, designed by Don Chadwick and Bill Stumpf.

Many of Herman Miller's products are branded with the designer's last name like the Eames lounge chair and ottoman launched in 1956 and are still in production today. The Eames lounge chair occupies a favored place in thousands of living rooms, studies, libraries, and dens, as well as in the permanent collection of New York's Museum of Modern Art. The chair, designed by Charles and Ray Eames, was named Design of the Century by Time Magazine in its final edition of the twentieth century.

Herman Miller's Resolve reinvents the very shape of office systems furniture. Gone are the right-angle paneled cubicles. They're replaced by versatile and inviting workstations at 120-degree angles. Space opens up. Air and light move through. People see each other. And the workplace harmonizes with change. It's the shape of things to come.

The Resolve system features full-width screens, multiple support arm heights, and additional poles to create a greater degree of enclosure for functions that require more privacy.

So beloved became the Beetle in the 1960s that Life magazine referred to it as "a member of the family that just happens to live in the garage." On February 17, 1972, the 15,007,034th Beetle was built, making it the most produced car in history, overtaking the legendary Ford Model T. It still holds that title today.

When you see a New Beetle parked on a street, no other car in the world looks like it, and the manufacturer's name instantly comes to mind. By reintroducing its classic Beetle in an aerodynamic look, Volkswagen has defied the automotive trends of the 1990s.

Drivers wanted

Those famous print ads for the classic Beetle of decades ago showed only the car with catchy theme lines like "Think small." That same approach to advertising can be seen in the print ads for the New Beetle, with the ad theme line "Drivers wanted."

Introducing the Volkswagen New Beetle in early 1998 was a high-stakes business gamble for Volkswagen's CEO Ferdinand Piëch. But it was Piëch who brought forth the management vision, courage, and determination to shape the New Beetle into a show stopper.

DaimlerChrysler. *Chrysler's PT Cruiser, with its unique retro ultramodern design, defied all of the auto motive design trends and became one of the most sought after cars ever produced by the auto maker. There are 26 combinations of how you can arrange the seating and back shelf in the vehicle's cargo area.*

McDonald's Signs Britney Spears and 'NSync

Teen boys can't get enough of heartthrob Britney Spears and teen girls go bananas over the 'NSync boys' band. So, McDonald's reached to male and female teens in its new TV spots featuring Spears and 'NSync performing together. The real pay off for McDonald's is in the merchandising of products bearing Britney and 'NSync's brand images.

Chrysler Gives Away a Free Swiss Army Knife

For Chrysler, the PT Cruiser has been a dream come true. To send a reminder of the PT's unique design, versatility, and durability, Chrysler sent out a free Swiss Army knife to 50,000 early inquirers. New product brand marketing doesn't get any better. And it underscores this point: When your product makes a connection with another brand slam product, you're only raising the bar higher for the competition.

BRAND SLAM MARRIAGES IN 2001

It's easy to tell the folks at Cuisinart that they should form a brand marriage with Chef Wolfgang Puck to market a new line of food processors under the Cuisinart-Puck brand name. But sometimes a brand slam marriage takes a gift of vision to see how dissimilar brands can tie the knot to create WOW in the marketplace. Here are my ideas for brand slam marriages in 2001 that I came up with to try to create WOW in the marketplace.

Cadillac and Bijan

I can envision a Cadillac luxury sedan co-designed with Bijan and marketed to well-heeled men in their forties and fifties. To build market share in the luxury car market segment, Cadillac needs to attract buyers in this age group. Today, the typical Cadillac buyer is male and in his sixties or seventies. If men's designer Bijan, whose core clientele is in their forties and fifties, had complete freedom to bring to life a new experience of what a Cadillac luxury car could be, it has to end up being WOW. Did you know that the English Bentley Azure in the color of "Sunburst Yellow" was invented by Bijan?

American Airlines and Chef Emeril Lagasse

God bless America if the day comes when you could get a three-course meal served on American Airlines that bears chef Emeril Lagasse's official stamp of approval. Now we're talking WOW.

Boy Scouts and Mrs. Field's Cookies

Millions of Americans look forward to that time of year when they can buy Girl Scout cookies from their kids or their friends' kids. After all, it's a good product and the profits go to support a terrific organization. But when you think about the marriage of the Boy Scouts' brand name with Mrs. Field's Cookies, it's got WOW written all over it.

Dunlop Tennis Balls and "Hill's Science Diet" Dog Food

My golden retriever Cosmos loves to carry a tennis ball in his mouth when I take him for walks down Broadway. Come to think of it, I never owned a dog or played with a friend's dog who didn't love to fetch a tennis ball. Tennis balls and dogs go together like bacon and eggs. Since Cosmos' favorite dry dog food is Hill's Science Diet, I offer this breakaway marketing idea to Hill's: Form a brand marriage with Dunlop to include an official Dunlop pro tennis ball in every 20-pound bag of dry dog food. I guarantee you've got a brand slam here and a big idea for a breakaway advertising TV spot and package design. Plus, there's the added motivation for dog owners to buy a several-month supply of your dog food.

LESSONS LEARNED

1. Form brand marriages with leaders in their categories, preferably those that rank No. 1.

2. The brand you endorse in your advertising should enhance your own brand.

3. The spokesperson for the brand you are endorsing should have the right image for your brand, too.

4. The brand you form a marriage with should be viewed as a brilliant marketing coup by your employees, customers, shareholders, and the nation's press.

5. Avoid a marriage with a brand that will create cultural or religious boundaries for marketing your brand around the world.

6. Most important, have fun forming brand marriages.

13

NOTHING BEATS
PRODUCT INNOVATION

Most companies aren't looking at their established brand-name products and asking: "What can we add, change, or do differently to hit a brand slam?" The bikini, introduced in France in 1946, was based on a simple idea: Reduce a woman's bathing suit to its bare essentials.

There's nothing like product innovation to hit a brand slam. And more brand slams were hit in the twentieth century through product innovation than in any other time in history. Then again, it was the century of mass production and TV and print advertising persuasion.

Our lives, our parents' lives, and our grandparents' lives were changed for the better thanks to the brand slam product innovations introduced in the last century. Here are a few worth noting.

- Paper Clip (1900)
- Zipper (1913)
- Frigidaire Refrigerator (1918)
- RCA Radio (1921)
- Home Air Conditioner (1928)
- *Life* Magazine (1936)
- Nylon Stockings (1940)
- RCA Television (1939)
- Tupperware (1946)

- Polaroid Instant Camera (1948)
- Xerox Photocopier (1950)
- Boeing 707 (1957)
- Procter & Gamble's Pampers (1961)
- Amana Microwave Oven (1967)
- Concorde Plane (1969)
- Intel Microprocessor (1971)
- JVC Video Recorder (1976)
- World Wide Web (1991)
- Pfizer's Zoloft Antidepressant Drug (1992)
- Cadillac's Night Vision (1999)

BRAND SLAMS COME IN SMALL PACKAGES, TOO

One of the smallest products to hit a brand slam in the twentieth century was M&M's bite-size milk chocolate candies packaged in a sugar shell. "It melts in your mouth, not in your hand" is one of the most memorable ad lines ever written in the chronicles of American advertising history. For all you trivia fans out there, M&M's is the No. 1 best-selling candy in America followed in rank order by Hershey's chocolate bars, Reese's Milk Chocolate Peanut Butter Cups, and Snickers bars. Did you know that 300 million M&M's are made everyday?

On the global scene, the plastic Lego block introduced in 1949, takes the gold hands down in the play product category. Invented by Ole Kirk Christiansen, a Danish master carpenter, Legos allow kids to snap the bricks together to create things of all types, shapes, and sizes. Most parents are quick to get bored with their child's play game. That's not the case with Legos, and maybe it's why more than 200 billion have been stamped out in the Lego interlocking design introduced in 1958. You don't need the media to remind consumers that you've hit a product brand slam when you've got Lego theme parks in the United States, Britain, and Denmark. Now that's WOW.

The Kodak Brownie, introduced in 1900, made photography an American obsession. Small, compact, easy to carry, and priced at $1 when it debuted, the Brownie hand-held camera was an instant brand slam with millions of people. Kodak could have given the Brownie away for free since it made its fortune selling the camera's film. Today, a mass-produced camera model that remains on dealer shelves for more than two years is considered a marketing success story. The Brownie was in production for more than a half century and millions of them were sold in all four corners of the world. After each picture was taken, you only needed to manually advance the film until the next film number appeared in a small circular window on the camera's back panel side. Unlike today's battery-operated digital cameras, the Brownie was fail-proof.

Another small product to hit a brand slam in the past century was 3M's Post-it Notes introduced in 1980. It's hard to imagine going through a day without writing a short note to a colleague, friend, or client; there's nothing more convenient than a Post-it Note.

Another miniature product that hit a brand slam was the paper clip, introduced in 1900. This bent-metal clip invention by Norwegian John Vaaler replaced the practice in the workplace of securing papers together by straight pins. Just think how many office workers have been saved bloody fingers thanks to the invention of this simple clip, which now comes in more colors than the NBC Peacock.[1]

A BREAKAWAY GAME SHOW

ABC hit a brand slam with its breakaway game show *Who Wants to Be a Millionaire* hosted by Regis Philbin, an American treasure according to CNN's Larry King. The enormous popularity of this innovative show increased ABC's ratings 16 percent in the summer 2000 season, and it contributed to a 45-percent rise in Disney's stock price when the show was at its peak. Here are a few lessons from *Who Wants to Be a Millionaire:*

1. If you're going to offer consumers a game prize, make it $1 million.
2. Select an advertising spokesperson that's a natural for your brand-name products.
3. Make your brand appeal to as large of a demographic base as possible.
4. Add drama in the stage setting and lighting of your product in TV spots.

PFIZER'S ZOLOFT OVERTAKES PROZAC AS NO. 1 ANTIDEPRESSANT

Pfizer, founded in 1849 by two immigrants, is known for being the company that introduces more new medicines than anyone else. It's a pioneer in the war against depression, diabetes, cardiovascular diseases, and many

---

1. *"Products of the Century" by Christine Chen and Tim Carwell (Fortune, November 11, 1999).*

other illnesses. Pfizer was the first to mass-produce the world's first miracle drug—penicillin. It was Pfizer's penicillin that saved so many lives in World War II. But the company's lifesaving chemicals go back further than that; they were used in the Civil War.

In the late 1980s, Pfizer's management retained my firm to name the company's new antidepressant chemical that would go head-to-head with Eli Lilly's well-established and then best-selling Prozac drug. At the time, the controversial Prozac drug for depression was a topic of discussion on almost every daytime TV talk show. While some called it a wonder drug, others claimed Prozac had altered their behavior in a bizarre way.

By March 2000, Pfizer's Zoloft overtook Lilly's Prozac as the No. 1 best-selling antidepressant in the world, with annual sales in the $2 billion range. The nighttime TV comedian Jay Leno remarked, "Now that Zoloft is the No. 1 selling antidepressant, the people at Lilly are on Prozac." The reason for Zoloft's sales success is attributed to product innovation—it has been shown to have fewer side effects than other antidepressant medicines.

Now here's how I coined the brand name Zoloft. The prefix "ZO" comes from the Greek word *zoe,* which means "life." The word *loft* means a "very high place." This implying a rise from a depressive state of being. I also wanted a brand name that wouldn't be confused with other drug names. Zoloft met that criterion since there was only one other brand name in all 42 trademark classes with the same prefix. But when you've got a blockbuster selling drug like Zoloft, it doesn't take long for other makers of medicines to copy your product name's prefix in the hopes that the magic will rub off. Today, there are some twelve medicines starting with "ZO."

GE's New Advantium Oven Hits a Brand Slam

General Electric is no stranger to product innovation. Its U.S. patents number in the thousands. In the late 1990s, its engineers came up with a "smart" oven that uses high-intensity light to cook food at speeds "unknown to mankind" as TV celebrity chef Emeril Lagasse might describe it. We're talking about roasting a whole chicken in fifteen minutes, or baking an Idaho potato in ten minutes—that's right, ten minutes, not an hour and fifteen minutes. And the end product looks and tastes better than if it were cooked in a conventional gas or electric oven according to the message delivered in the product's TV spots.

Such an innovative product deserves a great brand name and the folks at GE came up with one—Advantium. Obviously inspired from the word *advantage,* it also conveys a sense of state-of-the-art technology. Note the similarity in phonetic sound to Intel's Pentium brand name. Perhaps this wasn't by accident.

LESSONS LEARNED

1. Take a hard look at your company's brand-name products and ask if something can be added, changed, or done differently to make brand history.

2. Only introduce a new product if it's truly innovative when compared to well-established or best-selling products in the same category.

3. An innovative product deserves a great brand name.

14

BIJAN'S WINNING COMBINATION: A BIG IDEA AND ATTENTION TO DETAILS

Most companies devise a brand strategy hoping that in the process a big idea will emerge, which too often never materializes. With Bijan, the big idea comes first and then the brand strategy follows. Bijan has hit more brand slams than any other company out there, and he's done it with incredible style and taste.

It was early 1976, and I decided to visit Bijan's Rodeo Drive boutique. My office at that time was just a five-minute walk away from the most manicured and expensive three blocks of retail real estate on planet earth. At least, that's how I describe the Rodeo Drive experience to Europeans visiting Beverly Hills for the first time. I wanted to see for myself why this new Beverly Hills operation was the talk of the town in California magazine circles. Back then, Bijan's menswear collection was open to the public. A year later he would change that to "by-appointment-only."

When I arrived at the boutique's bronze and beveled glass Palladian-style front door, I was greeted by a white-gloved doorman dressed in formal white attire. Entering the store's foyer, I was greeted again by a receptionist. Wearing a classy off-white two-piece suit, she could have easily doubled for a *Vogue* cover model. She was seated in an ornate gold leaf upholstered arm chair behind a commanding French *bureau plat* with green marble inlays.

The receptionist jotted down the spelling of my name and called for an assistant. Very soon I was being escorted across an antique Persian rug and around a brass and clear Lucite centerpiece staircase to a private bar tucked discreetly underneath. "May I offer you a glass of Pellegrino, white wine, or champagne?" she asked. With a glass of white wine in my hand, this attractive and well-mannered woman in her late twenties continued the tour—pointing out a Baccarat chandelier of some 600 crystal pieces, the Italian and French armoires, a pair of stone dogs from an ancient Chinese temple, lush Hawaiian plants in large African baskets, and other treasures. Behind windowed closet doors hung an array of sport jackets, suits, tuxedos, and topcoats.

Every object in the store, both major and minor, seemed to have a reason for being there. There were no free-standing racks of clothes, or stacks of shoe boxes placed in corners or under tables. There wasn't even a cash register counter. Everywhere I looked there were statements of quality and extraordinary taste—reminders to Bijan's customers of the quality and detail that had gone into each finished tie, shirt, suit, and luggage piece branded Bijan.

A trim, attractive-looking man with dark-brown hair, chiseled face, and dark chestnut-colored eyes in a medium frame came forward to greet me with a warm smile. He was impeccably dressed. "I am Bijan, how may I be of help to you?" he asked.

After being overwhelmed by the ornate beauty of the store, I had to see for myself how great the customer service was. I wanted to see Bijan in action. "Do you have Italian-made shirts with medium-spread collars? I'm not into those Brooks Brothers button-down Ivy-league soft collar shirts," I replied with a tone in my voice, implying that I was a connoisseur of the fine Italian-made shirts.

"I understand what you want perfectly," he said. He walked around a long marble presentation table and removed about a dozen burgundy-colored shirt boxes from a large French armoire behind him. He opened each box and carefully removed the shirt inside as if it were a religious icon. Soon, a dozen shirts in different shades of blue, pink, beige, tan, and gray with white collars and cuffs were arranged side-by-side along the table for my inspection.

The shirts were spectacular. I was hooked. I had already known from reading a magazine article that the price of a Bijan cotton shirt was about $250 (and this was 1976).

Bijan left me for a moment. He returned with several tan- and beige-colored fine woven wool pants. He selected a shirt for each pair of pants. He then selected several dark-colored ties from the armoire, knotted them and placed each one under the shirt's collar to complete the "Bijan look." I couldn't help but notice that Bijan dominated everything and everyone in his boutique.

At Bijan's behest, I went into a dressing room to put on one of the shirts. When I came out, I noticed an intense expression on his face as his eyes scanned the shirt now draped over my upper body. "It's not right," he said, and asked his assistant to bring him the same shirt one size smaller.

When I stepped out of the dressing room the second time, I thought the shirt's fit was just fine. He called for the tailor and, with that same intense look, he pointed out minor alterations needed here and there.

I realized then that he wasn't just an ordinary merchant selling high-priced men's clothes. He was a perfectionist who really cared about seeing his customers look their best.

"How many shirts would you like to have delivered to you?" he asked.

I don't know why, but I wanted to push him even further, just to see how far he would go to satisfy one of his customers. I knew that if he came up with what I was about to ask him for, I would be writing a check to Bijan for about $6,000, plus tax.

"Bijan, I am leaving for a weekend vacation in Mexico. I need twenty-four shirts to take with me. Do you have twenty-four shirts in my size—any color, stripes, solids will do just fine?" I asked.

"Here are six shirts in your size," he replied.

I had him now. "Bijan, I never wear a shirt for more than two hours. In fact, I've got about a half hour left on the shirt I'm wearing. No, I must have twenty-four," I said. Bijan, noticeably eager to make such a big sale and please his customer, ordered his assistants to search the boutique from top to bottom for more shirts in my size.

"We've located three more," called out an assistant.

"Take the nine shirts," Bijan said.

"Bijan," I said, "here's my business card. Should you find twenty-four shirts in my size, call my secretary. It was a pleasure meeting you." We shook hands and I departed. I walked north to Little Santa Monica Boulevard to have a light lunch.

One week later, I went back to see Bijan. His warm greeting and the smile on his face told me that he admired my style. I purchased six shirts, two double-breasted sport jackets, several pants, and a few ties. So, in the end, Bijan actually came out on top. Plus, I was so taken by Bijan's style of doing "first-class business in a first-class way," that I featured him in one of my articles that appeared in *Advertising Age*.

It doesn't matter what business or industry you're in, or what brands you market—the story of this hugely successful Beverly Hills clothier, known for his men's fashion, perfumes, and outrageous print ads will inspire every marketer to hit a brand slam.

IT'S ABOUT IDEAS, NOT STRATEGIES

Bijan is not into strategies, strategies, and more strategies. His world revolves around ideas—ideas that bombard his brain from morning to night. When he gets one that fires up his creative juices, which is the root of every brand slam, he instinctively knows how to convert that mental thought into reality. No matter what he touches, he's a master at creating WOW.

FROM TEHRAN TO BEVERLY HILLS

Months after earning his degree in electrical engineering from a university in Switzerland at age 22, Bijan decided to change his career path. His desire to enter the world of fashion design prompted him to return in the early 1960s to his native country, Iran, where he opened a women's clothing boutique in a private home in an exclusive suburb in northern Tehran. Perhaps to be playful, or even controversial in those early retailing days, he named the shop "The Pink Panther."

The boutique's success prompted Bijan to open a fashionable men's store, which also did well financially. It gave wealthy Iranian businessmen a local place to buy fashionable menswear without having to travel to Paris, Rome, or London. In the 1960s, Bijan spent much time in Florence and Naples, Italy, studying fashion design.

By the end of the 1960s, Bijan was eager for a change and decided to visit America. He says he was shocked at the way many wealthy and prominent businessmen, professionals, and politicians dressed. No color coordination, trousers halfway up their ankles, baggy jackets and shirts, and wrinkled shirt collars. He concluded that his taste and design in menswear were needed here in the states.

In the 1940s, Rodeo Drive was a dirt road with only a few general stores. When Bijan moved to Beverly Hills in the early 1970s, Rodeo Drive was fast becoming the world's "Fashion Street." With financial backing from real estate mogul Daryoush Mahboubi, he purchased a parking lot on North Rodeo Drive and began the design and construction of a $2.2 million boutique. Bijan now had the prime location for his planned menswear operation. What he didn't have was brand-name recognition.

WHO OR WHAT IS A BEE-ZHON?

In 1974, during the time he was getting his boutique off the ground, it was difficult for him to find cooperation from people in the fashion industry or local businesses. The name Bijan in Los Angeles had no history or impact. The response from businessmen or bankers was: "Who or what is a 'bee-zhon.' "

When his store was within weeks of completion, Pacific Telephone requested a $200 cash deposit and a three-week waiting period before installing the boutique's phone lines.

In 1975, Bijan went to Europe to search out manufacturers to produce his own designs. He was often rebuffed because the Bijan brand name had no recognition. But he perservered, and today, business people, Hollywood agents and sport's stars are standing in line to form marketing alliances with the Bijan icon brand. Banks are eager to extend multimillion-dollar credit lines to his group of companies.

ATTITUDE-DRIVEN MENTALITY PAYS OFF

A ball player facing two strikes who hesitates for a split-second to swing at an incoming fast ball over the strike zone has just struck out.

Even before his Rodeo Drive boutique was open for business, Bijan developed an attitude-driven mentality that he was going to be the most talked about menswear designer around the globe. He shocked the established clothiers in Los Angeles and Beverly Hills with his declaration to the press that no one will sell menswear and accessories at higher prices than Bijan. To add more shock factor and attract media attention, he declared that Bijan menswear will never go on sale—something unheard of in the retail men's clothing business. If that wasn't enough, he later announced that access to his Rodeo Drive boutique would be by-appointment-only.

His critics and many merchants in Los Angeles said that by closing his front door to the public and demanding appointments, Bijan would be out of business.

Larry King recently asked Bijan on his CNN live talk show, "Who are your competitors?"

"I have no competitors," replied Bijan. "I'm in a league all by myself."

What's the lesson here? Take an attitude-driven mentality about your brands and don't hesitate to convey that attitude in your advertising and to the press.

CREATING WOW WITH PRODUCT PRESENTATION

One of Bijan's greatest talents is knowing how to present his menswear, jewelry, and perfume in a manner that magnifies their importance and prestige to the customer. In this context, three things stand out: The "House of Bijan's" location and its interior design and furnishings, Bijan's window display creations, and Bijan's magazine ad campaigns.

Location

Bijan's New York boutique on Fifth Avenue between 54th and 55th streets closed in February 2000. It wasn't because the Bijan empire couldn't afford to pay the $4 million a year rent on a new fifteen year lease. In *Women's*

Wear Daily, Bijan was quoted as saying, "Fifth Avenue is not for me any-more. The NBA store, the Disney store, Coca-Cola, Gap, and Banana Re-public are not the level of Fifth Avenue I want. The by-appointment-only operation I have deals with the most important men from all over the world. Why shouldn't I have my own building somewhere more fashion-able?" True to form, the "New House of Bijan" in New York will open in fall 2001 on Madison Avenue.

As for his Rodeo Drive boutique, after twenty-six years, Bijan decided it was time to renovate it. This was the very gem that rocketed the Bijan brand to heights unknown to any start-up men's clothier. According to *The Los Angeles Times,* the building's renovation cost $10 million. The original "House of Bijan" on Rodeo was WOW. The refurbished "House of Bijan" is double WOW!

The new Rodeo Drive boutique's entrance features a spectacular two-story glass and mahogany door. To the left of the door are thirty-six Spanish water urns, and on the right is a sculpture of Louis XIV, an icon figure of the most well-dressed man in European history.

Outside and inside this captivating structure Bijan brings together a palette of yellows and whites (reflecting nature and beauty) contrasted with accents of black cherry. Every piece of antique furniture in the boutique was handpicked by this maestro of brand marketing to reflect classic ele-gance in the Bijanian modernistic style.

What better way to remind his clientele of Bijan fragrances than to have all of the wardrobe closets and doors fitted with knobs that are actual Bijan perfume bottles? Always known for the unpredictable, Bijan's magnif-icent antique armoire at the back of the boutique leads to an oversized dressing room. Another prize is a painting by Fernando Botero, circa 1968, titled *The Rich.* While most fine art collectors would have selected a museum-quality gold-leaf ornate frame for the painting, Bijan opted to frame it on both sides with old French church doors to create a statement of WOW.

Bijan also was inspired to use $1 million worth of his crystal perfume bottles in varying sizes to create a chandelier that no one could duplicate. The perfume in the 1,000 authentic Bijan perfume bottles shimmers in bril-liant amber colors when the light in the boutique is on at night. To passersby on Rodeo Drive, it's a statement of Bijan WOW.

Window Displays

Bijan has hit many brand slams with his ideas for window displays. When tourists come to Beverly Hills, the locals often suggest that they do two things before returning home. First, visit Disneyland. Second, window shop along Rodeo Drive and neighboring streets and avenues comprising Bev-erly Hills' "golden triangle" of department stores, fashion boutiques, art gal-leries, outdoor cafés, restaurants, and nightspots.

For Bijan, turning one of his ideas for a window display into a statement of art is an expensive undertaking. A *New York Times* article[1] stated, "Bijan routinely spends $100,000 on his window displays to showcase his fur-lined cashmere coats . . . and his fine silk shirts." The cost today is double.

As busy as Bijan is running his menswear and fragrance empire, he continues to create all of his own window and showroom displays. After finishing a new window display, Bijan often spends an entire day changing or adjusting the items displayed, walking outside and inside perhaps fifty times to make sure each item is perfectly placed. "If a shoe, a shirt, or a coat is not just right to his eye, it will bother him all day," remarked his personal assistant Jayne Brandonisio.

Although Bijan attracts customers with little financial worries, he personally knows what it's like to be a stranger in a country with only enough money for a meal or a night's lodging. Memories of when he was a student in Germany and Switzerland have sharpened his awareness of "the man" underneath the clothes he's wearing. Often, this is expressed boldly or subtly in his window creations. His 1980 Christmas window is a classic example of Bijan WOW. Again, it had nothing to do with brand strategies, just a big idea that came to fruition.

In December 1980, Iranian militants were still holding captive some fifty Americans who had been assigned to the U.S. Embassy in Tehran. Their fate remained unknown. Christmas was nearing, emotions were building in the minds of many Americans for the government to take action against Iran.

Aware of the growing dislike by many Americans for Iranians at this time, and possibly because of it, Bijan wanted a window display that reminded passersby that in this world there is both the ugly and the beautiful. He still holds the hope that someday the ugly will vanish, and only beautiful people and things will surround us all.

He thought about the images that would convey these contrasting realities. Walking about his showroom, he noticed a pair of Italian-made leather shoes. Instantly, the contrasting images were clear, and he began a search to find hundreds of used army boots worn by U.S. soldiers in the Vietnam War. After weeks of searching, a source was located. The supplier couldn't understand why a men's clothier in posh Beverly Hills would want to purchase scuffed, worn, and weather-beaten army boots.

When the boots arrived, Bijan sent them out to be cleaned and polished. He wanted each boot to be seen as a beautiful vase. Each would hold a single fresh long-stem rose. Each day, a fresh rose replaced yesterday's rose. The visual message was awesome and powerful. Bijan had transformed a product used for war into a work of art and a symbol of peace for

---

1. Source: New York Times *feature article by Pamela G. Hollie, May 8, 1980.*

all nations, races, and religions. It was a brilliant twist on the biblical verse, "I shall turn your swords into plowshares." Bijan's glorious window displays never cease to amaze!

Fast forward to the year 2000. Another eye-catching window display created by Bijan featured huge posters of the presidential candidates, Al Gore and George W. Bush, with "Voting Is Fashionable" in graffiti-like writing. ABC News and CNN reported on Bijan's window display. Another example of WOW.

Magazine Advertising

Bijan has his hands in the creation and art direction of all magazine advertisements for his menswear, perfumes, and jewelry. From the start of his Rodeo operation in 1975 to the present day, "controversy" is a familiar theme in his ad campaigns. Although, at times, he simply focuses on a subject of beauty or innocence.

The creation of his new print advertising in 2000 was intended to pay homage to painters Peter Paul Rubens, Henri Matisse, and Fernando Botero. The ads feature a fully clothed Bijan and a decidedly large and rotund model named Bella wearing only high heels. *Talk* magazine was the first to run all three of the controversial ads—"Motel," "Siesta," and "Bella"— in its February 2000 issue. "Three days after the ads appeared in *Talk*, the representatives at some of the most glamorous New York magazines were calling me to say they would be delighted to run the 'Bella' ads," said Bijan.

According to Cynthia Miller, Bijan's art director, the public loves the ads depicting the full-figured nude woman. "Emails are being sent to me from around the world about the campaign. People are pledging to buy Bijan perfume for the first time just to show their support for full-figured models," said Miller.

Bijan also is famous for outrageous ads that feature himself—usually flashing a big smile or cracking up with laughter. There's an axiom in the advertising business: "Sex sells!" In one ad, we see the sexy Bo Derek flashing herself to Bijan and his young son, Nicolas.

I think Bijan is doing the right thing in taking center stage in his ads. What would you rather have hanging on your living room wall, a painting signed by Picasso, or a work purportedly done by the artist and signed by the studio of Picasso? The former might fetch $30 million at an auction. The latter might get you $10,000. Bijan is the artist and thinker behind his company's brand slams. His appearance in magazine ads reminds his customers that they're getting a signed Bijan, not a product signed by his studio. The great artists of the Renaissance like Leonardo and Raphael enjoyed their celebrity status, too. In public or in the palazzo's of Italian nobility, they were always surrounded by their admirers. In the twentieth century, artists such as Dali, Picasso, and Warhol were more than happy to step in front of the camera.

Hitting Brand Slams with Customers

Most of Bijan's brand slams are never seen by the public and are rarely mentioned in the media. Yet each is permanently embedded in the memory of his clients. As they say in the ad business, "No advertisement can beat word of mouth praise about a product or service experience." Bijan has been known to go far beyond what other clothiers would do to please their customers. When one client got a stain on a Bijan white leather jacket, Bijan had the jacket cleaned by a specialist in Italy at no charge. Another client, traveling in Europe, needed a coat for an Eastern business trip. Bijan—who keeps a file on each client's alteration requirements, likes and dislikes, the brand of scotch or wine he drinks, and the colors his wife or girlfriend likes to see him in—made the coat's selection and the necessary alterations. He then sent the coat by overnight delivery to the Asian hotel where the business executive was scheduled to stay.

Now allow me to speak from my own personal experience. It was January 1982. I was in the lobby of the Beverly Rodeo Hotel settling up my bill for a month's stay. I had made arrangements with a truck transport company to have my Cadillac Seville picked up near the LAX airport and delivered in seven days to my new residence in New York. Suddenly, it dawned on me that I had not removed and shipped the contents in my car's trunk—a newly purchased IBM memory typewriter, several Bijan jackets and shirts, and a large metal case filled with hand tools. "I'll never see these things again," I said to myself out loud. Then I thought: "Maybe I can leave them with Bijan and then arrange with a moving company to have them picked up and delivered to my New York apartment." I drove around the block, entered the service road running parallel to Rodeo Drive, and pulled into a parking spot near the rear entrance of Bijan's boutique.

I explained my predicament to Bijan. "Don't worry, I will take care of everything. Just write down the address that you want your things to be sent to," he said. Two people wearing white gloves removed my personal things from the car's trunk. I thanked him, said goodbye, and drove off. It would be many years later before I would see Bijan again.

About eight days later, the concierge in my apartment building called to inform me that a porter was bringing up three large boxes that had just arrived by UPS. "The shipper," he said, "was a 'Bee-Zhon' from Beverly Hills."

I opened the first box. Inside was an IBM white corrugated box protected on all sides by packing material. Inside the IBM box was my typewriter. I would learn later that Bijan instructed one of his assistants to find an IBM shipping box made for my typewriter model. Inside the second box I found my jackets and shirts. Each piece had been hand pressed, and the jacket sleeves had been stuffed with paper to keep them from wrinkling. Each jacket and shirt was placed in clear plastic wrapping. I opened the last box and there was my metal case also protected by packing material. When I opened it, I said to the porter who was removing the empty boxes, "Only Bijan would do this!" Each tool had been removed and carefully wrapped in white paper, and then replaced back into the tool case with more protective paper wrapping. Bijan never sent me a bill for all that he did to ensure that my personal things would arrive safe and in good order. Now that's what I call WOW in building a lifetime customer relationship.

FOCUSING ON THE PRODUCT

When it comes to the product, Bijan has a simple philosophy: "Charge whatever you want, but make it the best." He plays a strong role in the creation of his menswear collection and goes to great lengths to make it the best collection in the world.

Department store buyers of men's attire and accessories traditionally place orders for completely assembled goods on the basis of having seen the item in a fashion show, on the rack in a manufacturer's showroom, or illustrated in catalogs. In short, the buyer is relying on the manufacturer to produce a quality product made from quality materials. Keep in mind that the same mass-produced goods will carry the label of hundreds of different retailers, and will be sold to hundreds of different outlets worldwide.

Bijan is not in the business of producing raw materials like cotton, silk, wool, pearl buttons, gold thread, leather, and fur pelts that are used in his fashion designs. He is a designer, selector, director, and businessman who works closely with growers, ranchers, traders, mills, and factories throughout the world that are involved in the different stages of production to make the finished products that bear Bijan's label or his stamp of approval.

For Bijan, buying a shirt or suit without knowing the background of the fabric and tailoring that went into it is like purchasing a bottle of red wine with the label stating: "Produced and Bottled Somewhere on Planet Earth." The effort and the extra touches that he puts into his brand-name menswear collection comes through in these examples.

For starters, Bijan only selects the best crop of cotton in Egypt, where he says the finest cotton in the world is grown. Next, he has the raw cotton transported to selected Switzerland mill factories known for making the finest cotton cloth in the world. The bolts of finished cotton are then transported to a factory in Florence, Italy, where master tailors cut, sew, and detail the finished cloth to Bijan's designs.

When each shirt has been assembled, real pearl buttons are sewn in place. The shirt is then hand detailed, pressed by a craftsman who will finish, fold, and package the Bijan shirt in a specially constructed shirt box to protect the product from being soiled.

A black silk men's raincoat displayed in the window of Bijan's Rodeo Drive boutique could be four times higher in price than a raincoat made in England bearing a well-known brand label. The silk for the Bijan raincoat is purchased in China, dyed in Milan, and cut and sewn in Florence. The lining in the coat, also silk, is printed in a magnificent tapestry such as pheasants in flight. Upon closer inspection, Bijan has had his master tailor add concealed pockets for car keys and a passport. He concerns himself with only the fabrics and craftsmanship, and his designs and products reflect that concern.

HOW BOTTLED JUICE MADE BIJAN A GLOBAL BRAND

In the parlance of department store chain CEOs, the money is in "bottled juice." What they're referring to are the brand-name bottled perfumes and eau de toilettes (colognes) that dominate the main floor space of every department store around the world.

By the late 1970s, Bijan's flagship Rodeo Drive boutique was grossing approximately $12 million annually. The average customer was spending $5,000 per visit. The boutique's overall space was 2,800 square feet, so that came to annual sales of about $4,300 per square foot. The general manager of any department store today would be ecstatic to rack up annual sales in the men's department at $500 per square foot. Bijan realized that the target buyer market for his menswear line represented less than 1 percent of the world's populace. To build annual sales to $100 million and beyond, he would need to invent a new product line that appealed to men with a median annual income of $50,000 to $75,000. He had an idea. Market a Bijan perfume that sells at $1,500 for six ounces and bottle it in crystal made by the famous French Baccarat glass maker. Have each bottle signed and numbered, and insured against breakage. Then he would market to department stores and other retail establishments a more affordable Bijan eau de toilette for men in a bottle that resembled the original Bijan perfume in Baccarat crystal.

Michael Gould, chairman and CEO of Bloomingdale's, and a brilliant retail merchandising marketer, once told me that the cost to produce a 1.75-ounce bottle of a leading eau de toilette brand that sells in the $60 range is under $5. You're paying more for the glass bottle than the fragrance inside. In short, every successful marketer of fragrances knows that the bottle's design must be highly distinctive—a three-dimensional art form that people are proud to own and display in certain rooms of their home. Going with a standard factory-made fragrance bottle to cut down on the unit's cost is the "kiss of death" in the fragrance business.

Bijan hit a brand slam with his idea for a men's eau de toilette and a one-of-a-kind bottle design. The Bijan fragrance for men has catapulted the Bijan brand to global marketing stardom. On a personal level, it made Bijan a multimillionaire.

JORDAN BY MICHAEL IS A SLAM DUNK

Bijan is among the most successful designers in the marketing of colognes. In the mid-1990s he got the idea to partner a cologne deal with the legendary basketball superstar Michael Jordan. A deal was made with Jordan and Bijan for the designer to develop, design, market, and distribute two colognes under the Michael Jordan brand. Bijan's Michael Jordan and JORDAN by Michael are among the most successful men's colognes in history, according to the *Los Angeles Times;* sales reached $90 million in 2000. Jordan was personally involved in the fragrance formulations and bottle design selections.

Again, it took a big idea, not a strategic plan to achieve a brand slam with JORDAN by Michael cologne. Most marketers would have simply named the cologne Michael #23. Not Bijan, he had to put a spin on the name to create more WOW. The brand's name implies it's 100 percent "Jordan," and only "Michael" could pull off that slam dunk. Bijan went a step further to make the cologne capture the Michael Jordan aura by adding a black rubber sole to the bottle's base—a symbol for Jordan's breaking of NBA rules by wearing black Nike sneakers in official games.

NEW TWIST ON A WOMEN'S FRAGRANCE

Bijan's newest fragrance celebrates life's unexpected twists and turns. "Bijan with a Twist" will be available exclusively at the Bijan boutique and at Bergdorf Goodman in New York starting February 2001. "I wanted to create a women's scent that spoke to the twists in my own life, the feeling of being loved, not being loved, and being loved again," said Bijan. The designer predicted that his fragrance will make $10 million in retail sales in its first year.

As with all Bijan fragrances, the Twist bottle's design is unique. It's a chubby cylinder encased in movable gold bangles that surround the bottle. Each bangle is dipped in fourteen-carat gold, reminiscent of the famous childhood Slinky toy spruced up for the woman who wants some interaction with her fragrance gift. "A bottle with so much gold is very timely," said Bijan's daughter, Daniela Pakzad, vice president, creative services of Bijan. The stopper is an oval ring, which ties in with Bijan's signature loops.

While life's twists have their ups and downs, Bijan's package design for Twist focuses on the optimistic side. The packaging is a sunflower yellow petal box that's wrapped with gold cylinder ring wires and capped with a frill of raw paper inside. Now that's WOW.

BIJAN PAYS HOMAGE TO HIS CLIENTS

Soon after Bijan launched his menswear business, he looked for inventive ways to pay homage to his clients for allowing him to create their wardrobes. In the mid-1970s, he installed a crystal glass block wall in his Rodeo Drive boutique. On these crystal blocks were etched the names of Bijan's best-dressed clients. Over the years he has presented his list of famous clients in various themes in the display windows of his Beverly Hills, New York, and London boutiques. In his New House of Bijan, Beverly Hills, one will find leather-bound books—each with the name of a noted Bijan client. Some of these books contain up to forty or fifty full-color photos of the wardrobes and accessories that the designer created for that client. And inside each book are hand-written notes on what clothes and accessories to wear together for different occasions.

The books are a reminder to Bijan's clients that he works individually to achieve a distinctive look for each of them. It's this extraordinary effort to be there for his clients that keeps the most powerful and influential men in the world coming back to Bijan and more than happy to pay the prices this world-class designer commands.

When you make your customer look and feel very special to his wife, girlfriend, or business associates, you've hit a brand slam with him that he will never forget.

When I think of Bijan's phenomenal success, I am reminded of a copy line that appears in a Mercedes-Benz's 2000 TV commercial: "It's not always the price you pay for something, it's what you get in return." His supreme achievement may well be inventing Bijan. One thing is for sure, he's always raising the bar higher for himself and applauding his clients for doing the same.

LESSONS LEARNED

1. You create WOW by paying attention to details, details, and more details.

2. Raise the bar to a height that puts you far above the competition.

3. Only change something when you know you have an idea that will create more WOW in the customer's mind.

4. Keep surprising your customers with new breakaway products and an extraordinary service experience.

5. Never forget to pay homage to your customers—without them, you're out of business.

6. Launch ad campaigns that create WOW in the minds of your target buyers and the press.

7. All great brands begin with an unpredictable surprise, and they continue to flourish by reinventing more fun and adventure.

8. Forget about strategies—run with ideas that are daring, untraditional, and have WOW potential.

9. Think WOW!

15

BEETLE MANIA
ALL OVER AGAIN

Architect Frank Lloyd Wright once said, "What I like most about San Francisco is San Francisco." Likewise, what people like most about the New Beetle is the New Beetle.

In the 1980s, I fell in love with BMW's ad campaigns and the automaker's memorable brand slogan "The Ultimate Driving Machine." As I handed the BMW dealer a certified check, I said, "I hope this car is going to live up to its brand slogan."

His response, "Please, sir, the new BMW model you're buying is bulletproof."

"What do you mean by 'bulletproof,' " I asked.

"Except for regular scheduled maintenance, this car will never see the inside of my dealership's repair and service center," he answered.

Fifteen minutes later, driving my new Beemer south on the Hutchinson River Parkway, listening to Pavarotti sing *O Sole Mio,* the dashboard flashed a warning that looked to me like: "Stop engine immediately and get the hell away from the car!" It turned out that all of the oil in the engine had leaked out. As I watched the flatbed tow truck drive off with my new BMW and head back to the dealership, the words *bulletproof* echoed in my brain. About a week after I got my BMW back, on a cold wintry morning, I turned on the rear electric window defroster. Within a minute or so I heard an implosion sound. A thousand tiny glass pellets were all over my car's back seat and a chilling breeze was circling around my head and neck. As they were towing my new car away, I couldn't help but recall those words *bulletproof.*

The day I got my BMW back, three inches of snow were predicted that night in Westchester County, New York, where I lived at that time. I decided to park my car at the foot of my driveway for an easy escape the next morning. I soon discovered that my new BMW's rear wheel traction was about as effective in a few inches of snow as a horse with its hind legs tied together. Instead of backing out of the level blacktop driveway, the car eventually ended up in my front lawn. As they were towing it back onto the driveway, those words *bulletproof* once again rang in my head.

That same week I flew to Denmark to visit a friend who lived in the northern part of Jutland. A few days later, four feet of snow had fallen, and there I was in an eighteenth-century farmer's cottage right out of a Hans Christian Andersen winter wonderland story. If you had to drive; the only way to know that you were on the country road and not on some farmer's land was to follow the red-colored poles. They were sticking out of the snow next to the roadside. "How will we get out and shop for food?" I asked my friend. "Other than a few farm tractors, I haven't seen a car pass by on the road all morning."

"No problem," she answered, "I have a Volkswagen Beetle." Sure as the whiskers on a cat's face, that no-frills pint-size ten-year-old Beetle with a stick shift, roll-up windows, and manually adjusted seats got us around everywhere we wanted to go on heavy snow-covered roads. I recall her telling me that she paid about 5,000 Danish krone (equivalent to about $1,000 at that time) for her "Love Bug" when it was new. Meanwhile, my new $38,000 "Ultimate Driving Machine" was grounded in my driveway until the remaining icy snow finally melted away.

THE FIRST BEETLES

To understand the significance of the breakaway New Beetle car, you need to know some history about the most produced car in the world.

The first two Beetles arrived in the United States in 1949. They sold for about $800 each. The cars, which were simply called Volkswagen sedans back then, were far from being a hit with most Americans. In 1956, *Popular Mechanics* said this about the Beetle, "What is there about this small, ugly, low-powered import that excites people all over the world and makes every owner talk like a salesperson?" Yet, it wasn't until a few years later that consumer interest and emotional loyalty built up in America for the Beetle. There were logical reasons for this love affair with the car. For starters, it was now recognized as a marvel in German advanced engineering and the epitome of distinctive vehicle mobility. Second, it was a bargain price compared to the sticker prices of Detroit's big sheet-metal boxes on four wheels. Third, it was far less expensive to operate and maintain than Detroit's offerings. Lastly, the Beetle proved to consumers that they could be smarter than the Joneses by spending less, not more, on family transportation.

So beloved became the Beetle in the 1960s that *Life* magazine referred to it as "a member of the family that just happens to live in the garage." Some of the most brilliant ad campaigns in the annals of American advertising history had much to do with the cultlike adoption Beetle owners had of their cars. Volkswagen's "Think Small" ad campaign stands out as being one of the best. Another memorable ad showed the Beetle floating in water.

The Beetle's ride to the top was not without those unexpected bumps in the road, however. In the late 1960s, Ralph Nader and his consumer watchdog group declared the rear-engined, air-cooled Beetle as "one of the most dangerous cars on the road." What Nader and his followers learned the hard way was that once a brand is cherished by consumers, it's almost impossible to bring it down even if there's a huge product recall. Remember when the nation's press gave the "last rights" to Tylenol branded products after a few people died from poison-tainted capsules? Well, Tylenol not only survived the tampering shock and the biggest over-the-counter product recall in American history, its brand image is stronger today than at any other time before.

On February 17, 1972, the 15,007,034th Beetle was built, making it the most produced car in history, overtaking the legendary Ford Model T. Then on July 1, 1974, one of Volkswagen's plants, in Wolfsburg, Germany, ended production of the Beetle after thirty years and 11,916,519 cars—effectively bringing a twenty-five-year run of Beetle sales in the United States to a grinding halt. Production of the Beetle in Europe continued in Emden, Germany, and in Brussels. In 1981, the 20,000,000th Beetle was produced. On August 12, 1985, the last imported Beetles arrived in Emden. The Beetle left the European market, although production and sales continued in Mexico and Brazil.

Having sold millions of Beetles, why did Volkswagen discontinue the car's sales in America and Europe? While we may never know all of the facts that led to that remarkable decision, we do know that sales of the Beetle fell in the early 1970s due to an unprecedented assault on the U.S. market by Toyota, Datsun (now Nissan), and Honda. The automotive press declared the new Japanese arrivals to be superior in functionality, craftsmanship, and technology to any other competing American- and German-made cars on the road in terms of price. Many believe this was the reason why Volkswagen shifted strategy and put its U.S. advertising budget behind the Golf, Jetta, and Passat—three sensible, value-priced automobiles that Volkswagen thought could go head-to-head in design with the compact family sedans being built by the Japanese carmakers. As it turned out, the Golf hatchback, which essentially replaced the Beetle, never got to first base with American consumers. Regardless of reasons why the Golf flopped, the

Beetle was dead, and Volkswagen found itself in a big-time sales reversal. It was an emotional setback for loyal Beetle owners, who were not so eager to buy Volkswagen's new offerings.

Going through the minds of the company's U.S. executives was whether Volkswagen would join the likes of Fiat, Peugeot, and Renault and close up shop in America. At the same time, a big idea called "Concept 1" was cooking on the stove at Volkswagen's newly opened California design studio.

NEW BEETLE TIMELINE

January 1991—Volkswagen and Audi open a design studio in Simi Valley, California. Its mission is to explore design concepts that will support and improve each company's market position in North America.

September 1992—Feedback from the U.S. automotive markets convinces the design team, then headed by J.C. Mays, that the Beetle still remains the strongest product brand ever introduced by Volkswagen in the United States. The idea of resurrecting the Beetle in a reminiscent shape receives approval from Mays' boss Hartmut Warkuss at Volkswagen's headquarters. The California design team moves forward with the first of two 1:4 scale models.

March 1993—The prototype car, dubbed Concept 1, is presented in Germany to Ferdinand Piëch, Volkswagen's chairman and CEO, and he gives his support for the project. The decision is made to present a full-scale prototype car that people can sit in and drive at the January 1994 Detroit Auto Show.

July 1993—The first 1:1 Plastilin model of the Concept 1 car is completed.

January 1994—Concept 1 car is presented as a working model at the Detroit Auto Show. The car gets rave reviews from the auto press.

March 1994—A convertible version of Concept 1 is shown at the Geneva Motor Show. Ferdinand Piëch promises that Concept 1 will not remain just a vision.

November 1994—The Volkswagen Board of Management gives its approval to produce the Concept 1 car. Now Volkswagen's Wolfsburg design team, together with technical development engineers, takes on the serious task of making the idea that originated with the California design center a reality.

October 1995—At the Tokyo Motor Show, the Beetle-like car, now called the "New Beetle," receives a rapturous reception and 20,000 advance orders are received.

March 1996—The New Beetle is given its European premiere at the Geneva Motor Show. At the same time, Volkswagen goes on the Internet to reveal the New Beetle to the world.

January 1998—The factory-built New Beetle is presented at the Detroit Auto Show. It's one of the few models to go from design study to production.

A CALIFORNIA DESIGN CENTER'S BIG IDEA

Let me repeat what I said earlier: A big idea for a new product is going nowhere unless it's presented in a three-dimensional form that management can hug, squeeze, and caress. After the Beetle was discontinued in America and Europe, there had to be a number of Volkswagen executives who discussed the idea of bringing back a new version of the Beetle. But no one followed through on it. No one, that is, except Volkswagen's California design group, which took the idea to three-dimensional reality.

When J. C. Mays, then head of Volkswagen's California design center asked his chief designer Freeman Thomas what he thought about the idea of designing a new Beetle, the idea took root. Mays and Thomas submitted their prototype drawings of the Concept 1 car to their boss Hartmut Warkuss at Volkswagen AG, and Warkuss gave them the green light to go for the gold. But this new Beetle would, from an engineering standpoint, be nothing like the original Beetle. It would have front-drive, not rear-drive power. The engine would be mounted in the front of the car, not the rear. It would be liquid-cooled, not air-cooled. It would be a hatchback, not a two-door car. And it would be loaded with amenities unknown to the owners of original Beetles like air conditioning, a state-of-the-art sound system, power windows and steering, and an engine regulated by advanced automotive micro chip technology. What Mays, Thomas, and designer Graig Durley were most concerned about was retaining the iconographic look of the original Beetle, especially from the side view. And they accomplished just that. Now it was a matter of Hartmut Warkuss selling the California design studio's Concept 1 car to Volkswagen's chairman and CEO.

HIGH-STAKES GAMBLE FOR CEO

In the May 5, 1998, issue of *Business Week,* the magazine's cover story begins:

> Volkswagen's lovable New Beetle might have died an early death were it not for the fanatical ambition of Chief

Executive Ferdinand Piëch. In 1998, when VW was reel-
ing from a $1.1 billion loss, many managers viewed the lit-
tle car as an unaffordable plaything. One opponent,
research and development chief Ulrich Seiffert, went so
far as to hide the first full-size model from Piëch for two
weeks when it arrived at Wolfsburg headquarters from
VW's California design studio. But Piëch, whose grandfa-
ther had conceived the original Beetle, at Adolf Hitler's
behest, rolled over the naysayers, stuffed the car with the
technology he loves, and drove it to popular acclaim . . .

No matter what angle you study it from, introducing the Volkswagen
New Beetle in early 1998, was a high-stakes business gamble for Piëch. You
can imagine the egg on his face had the New Beetle bombed in America
and European markets within months of its debut.

I have stressed more than once in this book that hitting brand slams
takes people with vision, courage, determination, and talent. Volkswagen's
California design studio brought forth the product's idea and the talent
needed to execute that idea, which resulted in the breathtaking New Beetle design. But it was Piëch who brought forth the management vision,
courage, and determination to shape the New Beetle into a showstopper.
Even though Volkswagen's Concept 1 prototype car was tested with consumers in focus group sessions and at international auto shows from 1994
to 1996, it remained unclear to Volkswagen's management how people
would receive the actual production car in March 1998. Would there be
carryover brand loyalty from the retired Beetle to the New Beetle? This was
a question that could be answered only after the product's launch.

Volkswagen set a high goal of 50,000 unit sales in America over the
first twelve months. What it needed most was great critical acclaim for the
New Beetle and that's exactly what it got from the nation's car magazines
and the business press. Within the first eight months of the production
launch, American sales exceeded 50,000 units. New Beetle sales were so
brisk in the first year that there was a six-week wait for the car; the German
carmaker's Pueble factory in Mexico couldn't crank them out fast enough.
Volkswagen had hit a brand slam with its New Beetle in the biggest automotive market in the world.

The New Beetle is a marketing success story for Volkswagen based on
the simple idea of redesigning the "Think Small" car with aerodynamic
styling, safety advances, and an ergonomic interior, yet retaining the look of
the original Beetle designed by Dr. Ferdinand Porsche in 1935. It also was a
smart marketing decision to brand the redesigned car the "New Beetle" to
stress an all-new form of vehicle transportation for the twenty-first century.
Those that received the first arrival of New Beetles were selling them for up

to $3,000 over the car's sticker price. Volkswagen's brand slam coup dazed its competitors.

NEW BEETLE ADVERTISING HITS A BRAND SLAM

Those famous simple, honest, and quirky Beetle ads of the 1960s revolutionized Madison Avenue. One of the best ads showed a Beetle being towed. The copy line read: "A thing like this could happen, even to a Volkswagen. After all, it's only human."

So when Arnold Communications became Volkswagen's agency of record in 1995, it knew its Volkswagen ad campaigns would be measured against the simple and honest magic of yesteryear Beetle ads. The agency delivered the breakaway "Drivers Wanted" ad theme—an original new direction in automotive marketing, focusing on people who want to fully experience the act of driving. Like all great Beetle ads, "Drivers Wanted" is unpretentious about the brand, clearly communicating what makes the New Beetle cars different. "We think the New Beetle advertising will extend and strengthen our brand's appeal because it captures and brings to life all the magic, simplicity and originality that is Volkswagen. It is the emotional link between our brand's core values and customers around the world," said Liz Vanzura, Volkswagen's Director of Marketing/Advertising.

At the 45th Annual Cannes International Advertising Festival in 1998, a jury of twenty-two creative leaders in advertising, communications, and design from around the world chose the Volkswagen New Beetle print campaign as an international best, awarding it the Grand Prix for that category. It was selected as No. 1 from 7,000 entries from sixty countries. Ron Lawner, chief creative director and managing partner at Arnold, must have been a very happy man that day.

The group of thirteen print ads shows the New Beetle against a white background with witty copy like "0–60? Yes" and "Less Flower, More Power." From the very start in 1935, Volkswagen was out to achieve WOW by being the only carmaker to embody the concept of the "people's car." These ad campaigns developed by Arnold Communications enhance that concept 100 percent.

PRODUCT COLORS THAT KNOCK YOUR SOCKS OFF

Volkswagen's New Beetle and Apple's iMAC have this in common: Product colors that knock your socks off. The New Beetle comes in a dazzling array of colors; the paint itself has a metallic finish. This was definitely a brand slam with consumers.

A week after the new century rolled in, I had dinner at Joe Allen's, a popular haunt of theater and movie stars like Carol Bennett, Brian Denehy, and Al Pacino, located on Manhattan's Restaurant Row, with long-time friend Barbara Delano (no relation) who is a fine arts specialist at the renowned Tyler Graphics studio in Mount Kisco, New York. "I bought a New Beetle and I can't begin to tell you what a fantastic car it is," she said.

"You bought a yellow New Beetle, didn't you?" I asked.

"How did you know that, Frank?" she answered with a surprised look on her face.

"Tell me, is there a more dynamo-looking vehicle on the road than the yellow New Beetle?" I countered. She smiled back.

LESSONS LEARNED

1. Brilliant product ideas can be shown in sketch form in a matter of days, but selling the idea in rough form can take years. To shorten the time span, develop a full-scale working model of the product for top management to touch, hold, and caress.

2. Much of a new product's success depends on receiving critical acclaim of the product by the international press and industry spokespeople.

3. Never underestimate the power of a brand slam ad that captures the public's attention to your new product.

4. There can be magic in colors for new and reinvented products.

16

WOW PRODUCT DESIGNS FROM BANG & OLUFSEN

There are many people who buy products solely based on their design and the enjoyment they get from looking at these products in their home or office. For them, it doesn't matter if the product works; it's all about living with breathtaking product architecture. No one does it better in consumer electronics than Denmark's Bang & Olufsen.

Seven years after the end of World War I, Bang & Olufsen was founded by Peter Bang and Svend Olufsen in the town of Struer located in the weather-beaten northwestern part of Denmark. With 10,000 Kr. (approximately $1,500 in today's exchange rate) provided by their parents, they launched the world's first radio with mains plugs. Little did they know that in the latter part of the twentieth century their company's brand name would become synonymous with unique and exciting upscale audio and video entertainment systems and voice products for the home and office.

No question about it, product design remains the difference between Bang & Olufsen and its competitors. In 1978, the Museum of Modern Art held an exhibition of Bang & Olufsen's complete stereo and television product lines. This was only the fifth time since MoMA's opening in the 1930s that it exhibited the mass-produced goods of an industrialist. Since then, just about every museum of art and design around the world has displayed this Danish company's exquisitely designed products. To add to these exhibition laurels, numerous international design awards have been presented to Bang & Olufsen.

Bang & Olufsen has a long history of following its own instincts. Unlike many American old-economy manufacturers who can't seem to make a decision on any minor detail of a new product design without getting feedback from ten consumer focus group sessions, this company's designers and engineers make the call on what an entertainment system or soundspeaker should look like. Its breakaway product designs are matched by a company philosophy that stresses independence of mind.

SEEDS OF SUCCESS

Resourcefulness, cultivation of a team effort, and technological pioneering were the seeds of success for the nascent company. Concern for the product's aesthetics, respect for the interaction between man and machine, and the brand's visibility to global consumers have been added to its philosophy.

Bang & Olufsen has thrived in an industry so fiercely competitive that such giants as General Electric, RCA (the company that invented radio technology), and Westinghouse (which merged into CBS) were unable to sustain profitability in marketing their own brand-name audio or TV products. Despite their billion-dollar budgets for new product research and development, their legions of engineers and design specialists, worldwide distribution networks, and giant sales force, these companies were bested by European and Japanese companies.

It's ironic that those American family-owned businesses whose brands had become synonymous with radio, high fidelity, and TV such as Philco, Magnavox, Zenith, Emerson, Scott, Marantz, and Fisher (which pioneered high fidelity) have either sold their trademarks or trade names to Japanese companies, or they have gone out of business.

Even though consumer electronic companies like Philips, Sony, Panasonic, Yamaha, JVC, and Pioneer are many times larger in revenues and manufacturing output than Bang & Olufsen, this Danish company has maintained a technological leadership in its industry for more than seventy-five years. Today, Bang & Olufsen has approximately 2,350 dealers located in more than forty countries, and employs 2,700 people with the majority working in Struer where its headquarters and factories are still located. It's estimated that 82 percent of the company's production will be exported in the year 2001.

Since the early 1960s, Bang & Olufsen has perceived its role as the only manufacturer in its industry to offer people alternative products—products that are not only beautiful to look at, but easy to operate. Eliminating complexity and unnecessary gadgetry and knobs have become other hallmarks of Bang & Olufsen's products.

A Proud War History

The company's actions during World War II served to enhance its image in the eyes of its compatriots in the European community. It was a Bang & Olufsen engineer who devised a portable transmitter and receiver that enabled Danes to transmit uncensored news to London and vice versa. It took its name "The Telephone Book," because it was the size of a Copenhagen telephone book.

Because of its persistent refusals to produce products for the German army, it was difficult for the company to receive raw materials. That attitude (also made known in printed statements stressing Danish patriotism) and the fact that many Bang & Olufsen workers were involved in the Danish resistance movement, resulted in the demolition of its factory by German factory workers on January 14, 1945. Rebuilding efforts were begun immediately, which speaks to the resilience and resourcefulness of this proud Danish manufacturer.

Product Design Takes Root

As the story goes, a new outlook on product design at Bang & Olufsen was sparked by an architect's comments after he reviewed a Danish furniture exhibition in 1954. He described the furniture casings of radios and record players as having Norman arches and pot-bellied falsities with flourishes, hangings, and trappings composed of the most tasteless choice of wood, and plastered with plastic and brass trim. "Is it fishmongers and potato growers who in their spare time design these things?" remarked the architect in an industry journal.

The harsh review had an impact on W.L. Vindelev, the person then responsible for product development at Bang & Olufsen. He eventually concluded that the architect was correct, and decided to make some drastic changes in the way audio products would be housed in casings at Bang & Olufsen in the future.

The company's first stereo radio, Grand Prix Moderne 607, made its debut in 1960. It was housed in a simple, understated wood frame box designed to be placed on a shelf or mounted on a wall. Product design that would enhance a home's interior was now taking root in the company's mentality. The heightened interest in product design coincided with the introduction of the mass-produced and commercially available solid-state transistor, the formation of a European free trade association, and the entry of Jens Bang, Peter Bang's son, into the management ranks.

In today's world of Intel's Pentium III microprocessor, Microsoft Windows 2000, and Cisco System's operating systems to power the Internet generation, it's hard to believe that just four decades ago large electron vacuum tubes were standard equipment in manufactured radios. The transistor opened a new frontier in electronics and brought an end to radios and record players being housed in large pieces of furniture.

The company's Beomaster 900M receiver designed by architect Henning Moldenhawer was introduced a few years later. Fully transistorized, its integration of advanced technology and product design set a new standard that would be followed by other European and Japanese electronic manufacturers.

From this point forward, and through the visionary eyes of Jens Bang, product design would become the cornerstone of all Bang & Olufsen products. It's interesting to note that in the early 1960s, only three people in the organization spoke a language other than Danish or German. But the company's products themselves led the way for establishing the Bang & Olufsen brand in America and other countries.

Had it not been for Jens Bang, the company would probably not have designed and produced products in the 1970s that met the high standards for acceptance into the permanent collection of the Museum of Modern Art. He never asked his people to improve upon the shell design or technology of a successful competitor's stereo receiver, turntable, or tape deck. Instead, he challenged them to prove what these products should be—inside and outside. I recall Richard Latham, a long-time consultant of Bang & Olufsen telling me, "Jens Bang created the environment for product designers and engineers to explore the unknown."

KUDOS TO OUTSIDE DESIGNERS

The credit for many brand slam product designs goes to an outside industrial design firm or architect retained by a company. Yet, it's highly unusual for any industry giant to even acknowledge that it went outside for product design development, let alone to go out of its way to praise the design work of an outsider to the press, the public, its employees, investors, and suppliers. In America, one such company comes to mind—Herman Miller. You could almost say that Herman Miller has established a "Hall of Fame" to honor those outside geniuses who have designed the company's residential furniture, office seating, and open office systems since the 1950s. Many of its products are branded with the designer's last name like the Eames lounge chair and matching ottoman launched in 1956 and still in production today. Bang & Olufsen is another example of a company that's more than eager to give credit to its outside design chiefs.

Jens Bang recognized that the innovative products introduced in the mid-1960s would not continue to win over a sophisticated audience. To carve the company's niche in the home entertainment products industry, he recruited Jakob Jensen, product designer and a partner at Latham, Tyler

& Jensen, a Chicago-based industrial design firm. Jensen's mission was not only to design great-looking products but to design them in such a way that the music was more easily accessible for the listener.

Jensen's contribution to product design and function is exemplified in Bang & Olufsen equipment manufactured during the 1970s. He is credited for the design of the Beomaster 4000 turntable and tape deck, the Beomaster 1900 receiver, and the Beosystem 8000—which houses a receiver, tape deck, and turntable in one sleek-looking package. Bang & Olufsen then profiled the designer Jensen in its product brochures.

The integration of form and function is perhaps best demonstrated in Jensen's design of the Beomaster 1900 radio receiver and amplifier. All it took was a light touch of the finger's electrical impulse to cause the primary controls (such as sound volume, located at the front of the unit) to react. Secondary control functions were concealed under an aluminum hinged panel.

In the mid-1980s, others took the lead in the company's product development. But Jens Bang's philosophy to explore the unknown continues to this day.

AWARD FOR BEST PRODUCT DESIGN

Visit Bang & Olufsen's Web site (www.bang-olufsen.com) and you will find three pages devoted to David Lewis, the company's chief designer. The funny thing is, Lewis is not a Bang & Olufsen employee; he's a freelance designer. Visit General Motors Web site (www.gm.com) and see if you find any mention of GM's chief designer or the people who have designed GM division cars. Cadillac's brand theme is: "The Fusion of Design & Technology." My advice to GM Cadillac's management is to give tribute to the designers of your cars. Without their design contributions, the all-new Seville and DeVille wouldn't be among the top ten best-selling luxury cars in America.

While most designers work with pen and pencil to bring a sense of reality to their ideas, Lewis uses cardboard as his choice of medium to form his shapes for a new product. Lewis' thinking coincides with the point I made in an earlier chapter that you need to bring three-dimensional reality to a big idea if you want to sell that idea to management.

On one of its Web pages, Bang & Olufsen attributes the development of its anti-glare TV screen to Lewis. Irritated by the sun reflecting off his TV screen while watching a British football game one Saturday, he got Bang & Olufsen's concept development group to think about a solution to the problem. The anti-glare technology is now an important selling feature of Bang & Olufsen's TVs—another example of the power of a big idea.

Lewis' product designs including the BeoSound 9000 carry on a long tradition at Bang & Olufsen that people should control technology, not the other way around. The problem with new technology is that it opens up so many opportunities. Instead of making life easier, it often makes it more complicated because people have more options than they need," says Lewis. He goes on to say, "So many manufacturers are keen to use all the latest features of modern technology and make everything bigger and faster without necessarily making it better. I feel that many producers of home electronics are too quick to update their products. They improve the product 1 percent and relaunch it immediately—in many cases it would make more sense to wait until they had discovered some new features that consumers really need . . .[1]

NEW BRAND THEME: "A LIFE LESS ORDINARY"

According to Anders Knutsen, Bang & Olufsen's CEO, the new brand theme "A Life Less Ordinary" is directed at the principles that have always stood for the creation of new products. I can speak from personal experience when I say that Knutsen is "right on the money" with this brilliantly conceived brand slogan.

In 1971, the Museum of Modern Art in New York held an exhibit on the best product and furniture designs of the twentieth century. As I toured the show on the third floor, my eyes suddenly made contact with an audio system—FM stereo receiver and amplifier, record turntable, and speakers— that seemed to be a decade ahead of its time in design. All the components were housed in white cases, something I had never seen before by any audio producer. The FM receiver and amplifier were about three inches in height and had a brushed aluminum metal face. It didn't have any of those obtrusive knobs and gadgets to control functions. There were just two attached metal bars, each about one-inch wide, that moved across the aluminum face panel (similar in look to a slide rule) to control sound volume and to search for radio stations. The turntable's base was about one inch in height and the hinged, lift-up clear dustcover allowed the viewer to see the futuristic-designed turntable and record pick-up arm. The speakers were compact in size; their faces covered in a black fabric. I didn't have any comprehension of the system's inner technology, its power output, or the quality of the sound. All I knew was that I had to have this audio system. The name Bang & Olufsen appeared discreetly on each component's face panel in a Helvetica-like typeface and there was a crestlike insignia with copy that read: "By appointment to Her Royal Majesty's Court, Denmark." That at least told me the origin of the producer.

I returned to my office and began calling audio dealers in the Manhattan area. Not one of the store's managers had ever heard of this European

---

1. Source: Bang & Olufsen's Web site, May 2000.

producer's name. I called a dealer in Bedford Hills, New York, where I was living at the time and, low and behold, the owner was a Bang & Olufsen dealer and the store had in stock the very system I wanted. I recall thinking, "This is like buying a new white Corvette."

When my friends or relatives visited my apartment, they were immediately drawn to the design simplicity and elegance of my new audio acquisition. I must confess that I felt like my life was less ordinary now that I was living with Bang & Olufsen's stereo system.

Most electronic consumer products last about three years, five at best. My Bang & Olufsen equipment provided me with twelve years of sound enjoyment until I upgraded to the Beosystem 8000.

Unique and Exciting Products

To keep making it unique and exciting is the challenge that every manufacturer faces once it has earned a reputation with consumers, investors, dealers, and the media for hitting product brand slams. When you stop hitting them, your company could go into a nose dive. Case in point: The fashion brand Tommy Hilfiger has been under pressure since mid-1999. The company's stock has lost in twelve months about 75 percent of its market cap valuation as of April 2000. Four years ago, this brand was the darling of Wall Street and its stock price was flying high. The designer's brightly colored casual women's and men's clothing designs were grabbed up by millions of college students and others in their late twenties and thirties who wanted to identify with the trendy Hilfiger designer brand. So what went wrong? One financial analyst had this to say: "Uniqueness and excitement are what drive the sales of designer-label clothes to a youthful market, and Hilfiger seems to have lost his magic lately."

When you look at Bang & Olufsen's product portfolio over the past thirty years, the company has done a remarkable job of introducing new audio, video, and communications products that indeed excite the senses. In fact, it has done such an excellent job that it has created a market for Bang & Olufsen knock-off design products made in Asia and sold in discount electronic shops at much cheaper prices. Of course, Chanel women's bags, Rolex men's wrist watches, Mont Blanc writing pens, and Ralph Lauren sunglasses, among other brand-name designer products, have been knocked-off for decades. There's not a major city around the world where you won't find these look-alike products sold by unlicensed sidewalk peddlers. These copycat products are a billion-dollar industry.

A prototype car design sculptured in clay is one thing. Manufacturing that car in sheet metal and plate glass to look just like the prototype is another thing. Ole Terndrup, Bang & Olufsen's concept developer knows this all too well. Aside from design, what makes Bang & Olufsen's products special are the materials, manufacturing fabrication, and finishing that go into the product. Therein usually lies the difference between the genuine brand-name product and its knock-off cousin.

Most old-economy companies have their chief product designer reporting to the chief of marketing and sales. It's the top sales people who have the last say on what the new product's content, form, and function will be. Not so at Bang & Olufsen—the chief designer is the conductor of the new product's orchestration. Engineers and manufacturing specialists work through his ideas. Now, if you're the CEO of a manufacturing company who has never hit a brand slam product design, maybe it's time to make the chief designer (whether inside or outside) do what he or she knows best—design the product.

I stress repeatedly in this book that it takes a big idea to hit a brand slam, not strategies, strategies, and more strategies. Bang & Olufsen is proof of that. A project starts when an idea is sold to management. Then people from design, engineering, manufacturing, marketing, and administration come together to form the orchestra that will bring reality to that idea. Says Knutsen, "If we can define a product in one sentence, then we know it is ready to be introduced. A precise definition of a new product almost always originates from the manufacturer. It is unlikely to come from an advertising agency." That's the process this Danish manufacturer follows to hit a brand slam.

DESIGNS THAT GO THE DISTANCE

Bang & Olufsen's designers push the design envelope to the edge in search of product designs that last at least ten years. The Beosystem 8000 looks like it was designed today, not two decades ago.

CEO Knutsen's favorite product design is the BeoSystem 2500 designed by Lewis. Unlike the anonymous Japanese-made black boxes that house CDs, Bang & Olufsen has opted for an upright design that highlights the CDs so that you can read the song title on them. It's just one more example of a breakaway music system.

In the automotive industry, a new car is doomed from the start if it's not a decade ahead in design. The design (referred to as the "jelly bean" by the auto press) of the first generation Ford Taurus launched in 1986 lasted about ten years before noticeable exterior and interior design changes were made to the product line. Chevrolet's two-seater Corvette sports car has undergone several radical design changes since its introduction in the mid-1950s. Yet, GM's designers have managed to keep the Corvette ten years ahead in design look in every production. In contrast, when Oldsmobile launched an all-new version of its entry-level Calais car in the 1991 model year, the car's design already looked dated when the first manufactured unit rolled off the assembly line. It came as no surprise to many auto analysts when production of the car was halted after three years due to lackluster sales. This futuristic approach is what keeps Bang & Olufsen pioneers in business.

In the book *In Search of Excellence,* authors Thomas J. Peters and Robert H. Waterman, Jr., make this point: "The excellent companies have a deeply ingrained philosophy that says, in effect, 'respect the individual,' 'make people winners,' 'let them stand out,' 'treat people as adults.' " Bang & Olufsen talks endlessly about the individual's contribution. CEO Knutsen remarks, "It's a team concept here; we make the most of every team member's talent to produce a product that lives long after the whims of fashion have lost their attraction. Our people are proud of their company and the quality products they take part in producing. We have people working here as third generation Bang & Olufsen employees."

LESSONS LEARNED

1. Harness the power of design to make people's lives less ordinary.

2. Push the design envelope to the edge; develop product designs that can last at least ten years.

3. Don't allow consumers to dictate the design of your new product or you will more than likely end up with another me-too product.

4. If you can define a new product in one sentence, then you know it's ready to be introduced.

5. Give your designers credit for product design excellence, make them winners, and praise their accomplishments. Remember, these are the people who can catapult your company's new product to marketing success with a WOW product design.

6. Cultivate a team effort to bring design and technological innovation together.

7. Let product design bring the person and the machine closer together.

17

OGILVY & MATHER'S BRAND SLAM CAMPAIGNS

"Every advertisement is part of the long-term investment in the personality of the brand."

David Ogilvy, 1955

D avid Ogilvy, in my mind, is *the* greatest ad man of the twentieth century.

I don't recall the actual day, but it was in July 1983, that I spent several hours interviewing Ogilvy at Ogilvy & Mather's old offices at 2 East 48th Street, New York. It was hard not to notice the wall-to-wall red carpeting on every floor.

It would be the first of three interview sessions that I would have with Ogilvy over the course of two weeks. He was gracious enough to grant me eight hours of his time to hear his thoughts on what it takes to build great consumer brands.

Being such a legend in the ad world, I was expecting to be greeted by a man with the physique of John Wayne. Instead, Ogilvy looked more like the late Douglas Fairbanks, Jr.—a small, trim, distinguished-looking man with a full head of grayish-brown hair. He was seventy-two, but he carried himself like a man ten years younger.

Ogilvy was wearing his signature red trouser suspenders and striped red shirt. And, of course, there was his pipe resting inside a crystal glass ash tray on the table. Having met a number of prominent advertising professionals in my career, I began to wonder if this guy was an egomaniac or a slick, homogenized politician. He was neither. The fact is, he was very reserved and more of a listener than a talker, which hit me with considerable impact since he built his fame from generating words. He had hand-picked the flamboyant and charismatic Jock Elliott, a man with a bearlike frame, to preside over the agency as chairman.

As our discussion progressed, he seemed more interested in hearing my thoughts about building great brands. I would learn later that he was writing an article on how to build powerhouse brands.

"I can see you like the color red," I said.

"Yes, it does make a memorable impression," he answered.

"David, do you know why the pope only allows cardinals to be adorned in red habits?" I asked.

"No," he replied.

"It's to remind them that they must be prepared to shed their blood for their faith."

"Very interesting," he said. "I'm making a note of that for my next speech to our shareholders and Wall Street analysts."

I pulled out his book *Confessions of an Advertising Man* from my briefcase and placed it on the table. "It's a fascinating read," I said.[1]

"I never thought this book would sell more than 4,000 copies. It's turned out that several hundred thousand copies have been sold to date in both hardcover and paperback. The royalties have more than covered my son's Ivy-league college tuition and his room and board," he said with a noticeable smile breaking on his face.

During all of our discussions, Ogilvy never once bragged about himself or about his accomplishments. Instead, he talked about his beloved agency and the capable people who worked there at the time including Jock Elliott, William Phillips, Michael Ball, Norman Berry, and Hal Riney, and how their talents, dedication, and hard work built a world-class agency brand. I was taken by his remark that he considered Hal Riney, then creative director of Ogilvy's San Francisco office, to be a better copywriter than he ever was during his heyday. Riney eventually left Ogilvy to form his own agency, Riney & Partners.

Ogilvy stressed the importance of producing a genuine selling idea in an ad campaign. He firmly believed that great advertising has identifiable qualities, and once you're aware of these qualities, you stand a better chance of creating the most successful advertising in your industry. I will always be grateful to him for sharing his knowledge and for shaping my thinking on the importance of creating WOW in brand marketing.

Ogilvy also emphasized the importance of being recognized by advertisers as an agency that does first-class business and treats its people with ci-

---

1. *David Ogilvy's book,* Confessions of an Advertising Man, *was published in 1963 by Atheneum Books, New York. While it's out of print, it can be special ordered on audiocassette for about $60.*

vility. This was evident in himself and the people he had selected to run the agency he founded. "There are no positions available for bullies here," he noted. "But that doesn't mean we're pussycats either."

"I've seen large barking dogs back away from a fight with a kitten." I said.

"Come to think of it, dynamite does come in small packages," he replied.

By the end of the third interview session, it was quite obvious that David Ogilvy was to the core of his being an "ad man." And if that's what he wanted others to remember him by, he certainly got his wish.

DAVID OGILVY'S LEGACY

My office is one block north of Ogilvy & Mather's worldwide headquarters located in the Worldwide Plaza building at 49th Street and 8th Avenue. Each time I walk my golden retriever Cosmos past the agency's lobby entrance, I instinctively turn my head to look at the Ogilvy logo—David's own signature—appearing in black on a large rectangular red sign, which is mounted above the long, dark-gray granite and marble reception desk. On the far wall to the right is a gigantic black and white photo of a contemplative-looking Ogilvy in his signature striped shirt and suspenders.

Ogilvy died in 1999 but he left a legacy to his agency's heirs and to the advertising profession. The smartest thing that Sir Martin Sorrell, group chief executive of the WPP Group, did when he acquired Ogilvy & Mather was to keep David Ogilvy's brand identity in place as well as his principles for hitting brand slam campaigns.

Sir Martin Sorrell had this to say, "David Ogilvy was the subject of countless affectionate and respectful tributes from around the world. He had earned every one of them . . . He had created and inspired advertising campaigns which set new standards of style and effectiveness. To clients and competitors alike, he swiftly came to epitomize the very best of the advertising industry . . . His books are still widely read, and the company he built has never been in better shape. We may be absolutely certain that, together, they will serve as his rightful and enduring monument."

When the *Wall Street Journal* recently asked Rick Boyko, a chief creative officer at Ogilvy & Mather North America, for his thoughts on brands, Boyko said, "Our job is not just to make brilliant ads, but to create advertising that sells within the character and context of the brand. That was David Ogilvy's vision. It still holds true for clients the likes of which he never imagined, such as the Internet-based companies . . ."[2]

---

2. Wall Street Journal, *"Adventures in Capitalism" ad campaign, 2000.*

Boyko's reference to David Ogilvy is not atypical. When you talk to the top people at Ogilvy & Mather, it's almost impossible for them to discuss brand advertising without bringing the agency's founder into the conversation. The ability to keep Ogilvy's tenets alive and flourishing among a workforce now numbering almost 10,000 is crucial to the success of this agency with a worldwide reputation for coming up with big campaign ideas and smart, well-tailored work that builds strong brands.

What makes Ogilvy unique among other big agencies—including its sister agencies J. Walter Thompson and Young & Rubicam—is that it has succeeded so well in building its own brand and defining that brand's personality and heritage to the media and the business world. The high standards of its advertising creations for its clients are a reflection of its own inner soul.

As he notes in his book, when he launched his agency in 1948, Ogilvy told his staff of four people, "Agencies are as big as they deserve to be. We are starting this one on a shoestring, but we are going to make it a great agency before 1960."[3] By 1960, the staff was 247 strong. From 1960 to 1980, the agency's billings jumped from $32 million to almost $2 billion worldwide. It went from a small New York office to having 134 offices in 34 countries. In 1989, the WPP Group, based in London, achieved a major coup by acquiring the best brand in the ad business. In 1999, Ogilvy & Mather Worldwide ranked tenth among global agencies and had 359 offices in 100 countries.

Aside from creativity, the characteristics that have supported Ogilvy & Mather's phenomenal growth are aggressive business development, careful financial management, and the continued pursuit of advertising knowledge. For five decades to the present day, Ogilvy & Mather built lifetime value with its clients by not straying far from the core principles its founder put in place. Look at what can happen when management doesn't pay attention to the principles that built a company's empire.

In 1998, the parent of F.W. Woolworth Company announced that all Woolworth stores (about 400 in America) were closing their doors. For 117 years, the Woolworth store was a fixture on America's urban landscape. It was a place where shoppers could find an array of general household and personal items at a fair-value price, as well as a place to have lunch or an ice cream float at the store's soda counter. So what brought about the downfall of this famous retailing brand icon? There are a number of reasons. For one thing, management lost sight of the founder's vision that every Woolworth store in America be a friendly, fun, clean, and up-to-date place to shop in. In contrast, H.J. Heinz remains a powerhouse today because every succession of management has respected and adhered to the quality guidelines set down by H.J. Heinz himself.

---

3. David Ogilvy's Confessions of an Advertising Man *(Atheneum Books, New York).*

In the 1870s, dirty floors, unclean work areas, foul-smelling employee break rooms, and bugs and vermin were considered a way of life in most food-processing factories. When H.J. Heinz opened his first factory, he refused to accept such intolerable practices. He demanded that his factory managers maintain strict sanitary codes for food handling and that the factory be kept sparkling clean. He insisted that all factory workers wash their hands vigorously with soap and hot water after having visited the toilet. The press soon heard about Heinz's fanatical obsession for factory cleanliness and the news coverage scored a PR brand slam for the emerging food company known for its variety of bottled pickles.

DOING FIRST-CLASS BUSINESS IN A FIRST-CLASS WAY

In 1983, I interviewed William Phillips, Ogilvy's then U.S. president and CEO, for his thoughts on why Ogilvy was such a brand force in the ad business. He said, "From the very beginning, we have conducted 'first-class business in a first-class way.' I feel this is perhaps the single most important ingredient of our success so far." Phillips himself was an example of one of Ogilvy's doctrines: Always try to promote from within. Phillips started at Ogilvy as an account manager of Maxwell House coffee back in 1959 and gradually worked his way to the top.

"What do you mean by doing first-class business?" I asked Phillips.

"In the ad world, this is the opportunity to work for industry giants to create memorable ad campaigns that more than accomplish their objectives," he answered.

Some of the most successful ad campaign themes in the 1970s were created by Ogilvy. Here are three such brand slams for its clients.

1. **Shell's "Nine ingredients for top performance."** This ad campaign helped rocket Shell from seventh to second in market share ranking in just a few years following the new brand's positioning in TV commercials.

2. **The Smith Barney campaign, "They make money the old-fashioned way—they earn it."** Built around veteran actor John Houseman, this one put Smith Barney on Wall Street's center stage. Some thirty years later, a version of this ad theme line, created by Ogilvy & Mather, is being aired under the Salomon Smith Barney brand. How many brand ad themes can boast that kind of mileage?

3. **The "Do you know me?" campaign promoting the American Express Green Card.** The ad theme line, parodied by Johnny Carson on *The Tonight Show*, and by the cast of *Saturday Night Live*, became part of the American culture. It even inspired

cartoons in *The New Yorker.* More important, it tremendously increased card membership in the Green Card. Want proof? In 1974, when the TV ad spots first aired, there were 3 million card members and only eight people working at American Express on the Green Card business. By 1980, there were 10 million card members and 200 people working in the Green Card division.

Ogilvy's recent brand slam ad campaigns include the following:

- **"Dream with Your Eyes Wide Open."** The print ad theme reminds young girls of the most prized play doll in the world, Barbie.
- **"The Greatest Risk Is Not Taking One" ad campaign.** This underscores AIG's businesses—insurance and financial services.
- **"Stunning Looks and Brains Too" ad campaign.** This reminds us that the new American Express Blue Card has a built-in chip for added fraud protection.

ROOTS, AND BRANCHING OUT

From the beginning of the agency's growth, Ogilvy had a vision of the clients he wanted most: General Foods, Bristol-Myers, Campbell Soup Company, Lever Brothers, and Shell Oil. Eventually, all five became clients of Ogilvy. As the years passed, he continued to surround himself with accounts that helped ignite his creative juices including Rolls-Royce, Schweppes, Hathaway, and Steuben.

Following Henry Ford's advice to his dealers that they should "solicit by personal visitation," Ogilvy got his start soliciting advertisers who did not employ an outside ad agency, believing he lacked impressive case studies to win the job. His first target, as he tells in his book, *Confessions of an Advertising Man,* was Wedgwood China, which at the time had an annual ad budget of $40,000.

While Hensleigh Wedgwood and his advertising manager received Ogilvy with much respect, they considered an ad agency more trouble than what it was worth. Still, they showed him the company's ads and asked for his opinion.

Ogilvy's response was that he liked them, and he asked if they would allow him to buy space for Wedgwood. It wouldn't cost the company anything and he would receive the media commission from the magazines. Ogilvy's straightforward talk had its impact and the next day Wedgwood wrote him a formal letter of appointment. Bingo! The Ogilvy advertising agency was born.

The $6,000 capital to start the ad agency, however, was not enough to keep the Ogilvy agency afloat until the first Wedgwood commission arrived. Fortunately, Ogilvy's elder brother, Francis, was then managing director of Mather & Crowther, a noted ad agency in London. Francis convinced his partners to back his brother's cash flow needs and to lend him the Mather name for added image prestige.

Bobby Bevan of S.H. Benson, another English agency, followed suit. Overseas investments were completed and the trade name of Ogilvy, Benson & Mather was now on record with the trade press in America.

The agency's new investors were concerned that an Englishman, or even a Scotsman, would have a difficult time persuading American companies to give him any advertising business. Ogilvy was advised to hire an American to head the fledgling agency. So he convinced Anderson Hewitt to leave the Chicago office of J. Walter Thompson and become his boss.

Hewitt had many connections with top management and within a few years he managed to bring in three big accounts—Sunoco, Chase Bank, and Hathaway. In 1953, despite the agency's meteoric rise, Hewitt resigned and Ogilvy again took the helm of the agency he founded.

REACHING THE IMPORTANT AUDIENCES

In the early 1950s, Ogilvy was competing with heavyweight ad agencies. A true maverick, he invited reporters from the advertising trade press to a luncheon. He told them of his ambition to build a major agency from scratch. And, as he tells in his book, the press gave him priceless tips on advertisers looking for a new agency. His news releases were always picked up by these reporters. Believe me, it's a lot harder today to win such admiration from the trade press.

In one speech to the advertising community, Ogilvy denounced advertising education in America, and offered $10,000 to help start a college of advertising that would issue licenses to practice. It created a stir back then on Madison Avenue (the reference to Madison Avenue is no longer accurate since most agencies have long since fled this high-rent district, including the Ogilvy agency), and made the front pages. Soon reporters sought out Ogilvy for his comments on major advertising news.

He made friends with men and women whose jobs brought them into contact with major advertisers, researchers, public relations consultants, management advisors, and media moguls. These people also saw in Ogilvy a possible source of future business for themselves, but what they got was a selling pitch on his agency's ability to create the most successful advertising in America.

He was one of the first to mail out progress reports to people in every walk of life. Even the most seasoned advertisers looked forward to reading this insightful information.

The people who worked with Ogilvy will tell you that he was always an originator, developing his agency through a pragmatic, hands-on approach to determine the directions in which success for his clients were made possible. He was not a follower of popular creative trends and fashion in the ad business. "This attitude is very much alive today at Ogilvy," said Bill Gray, president of Ogilvy & Mather, New York.

Ogilvy may well be the first advertising professional in American history to show prospective clients the dramatic improvement that followed when his agency took accounts away from other agencies. His agency always blazed new trails, and in every case increased the brand's market share.

GOING AGAINST THE TIDE

Historically, when a company decides to change its ad agency, it invites various firms to create speculative ad campaigns to show how they would position the company's flagship brand. Ogilvy was the first to go against this practice and he succeeded in winning accounts on his agency's brand reputation. The KLM account is one such example.

In the 1950s, KLM Royal Dutch Airlines invited Ogilvy and four other agencies to make speculative campaigns. Ogilvy was the first on KLM's tour of inspection. After greeting KLM's management team, he said, "We have prepared nothing. Instead, we would like you to tell us your problems. Then you can visit the four other agencies on your list. They have prepared speculative campaigns. If you like any of them, your choice will be easy. If you don't, come back and hear us. We will then embark on the research that always proceeds the preparation of advertisements in our agency." Five days later, the Ogilvy agency was retained by KLM.

BUILDING MANAGEMENT DEPTH

In 1957, Ogilvy wooed Esty Stowell to join his agency. Stowell had been executive vice president of Benton & Bowles, which was widely regarded as one of the best ad agencies in brand marketing. His marketing background proved to be the big gun the agency needed to reach the next plateau. Ogilvy had already established his agency's reputation as America's No. 1 agency for inventing brilliant print advertising headlines. "At sixty miles an hour, the loudest noise in the new Rolls-Royce comes from the electric clock," scored a brand slam for the British carmaker.

Stowell's good management skills convinced Ogilvy to turn over to him the responsibilities of every department in his agency except for creative. From that point on, the agency began to grow in bigger chunks, and Ogilvy became an agency strong in brand marketing.

In 1960, Jock Elliott, an account executive and director at BBDO, was recruited by Ogilvy to manage the Shell account, which had the biggest billings at Ogilvy at that time. On December 10, 1965, in the auditorium of MoMa, where Ogilvy had assembled his people for an annual event, he announced the appointment of Jock Elliott to chairman of Ogilvy U.S. In the same year, Ogilvy became chairman and creative director of the newly named parent company Ogilvy & Mather International. And Ogilvy, Benson & Mather New York and Mather & Crowther changed names to Ogilvy & Mather. On April 27, 1967, Ogilvy & Mather International became the first ad agency to go public on the New York and London Stock Exchanges.

I interviewed Jock Elliott, then chairman emeritus of Ogilvy & Mather, on three occasions in the summer of 1983. After hours of listening to him praise David Ogilvy, it was easy to see why Ogilvy considered him to be a good and trusted friend. Elliott, an amusing and witty man, also had a fetish for bright-colored trouser suspenders, bold striped English-made shirts, and a good pipe smoke. He was the consummate ad account manager as reflected in his polite English mannerisms and choice of words. I tried my best to get him to tell me a juicy story like how the agency blew a major account out of stupidity and all I got was more praise about Ogilvy.

ADVERTISING THAT SELLS

In the 1960s, Ogilvy accused the New York advertising community of pursuing gold medal awards instead of building sales for its clients. He noted that the vast number of ad campaigns that won Clios (the Oscar in the ad world) did little to sell the actual product advertised—the only winners he said were the three national broadcasting networks and media giants.

Aware of the growing frustration among corporate CEOs in assessing what was wrong with their company's advertising campaigns, Ogilvy set out to measure the effectiveness of campaigns created by his agency. The results of this undertaking—at a considerable cost—enabled the Ogilvy agency to identify techniques that increased the selling power of advertising, as well as techniques that decreased their selling power.

The agency's research people had amassed thirty-two items of substantive information. Ogilvy believed that if he packaged and promoted this information in a convincing way, it would make his agency stand apart from the competition. He created a slide presentation, which he named "Magic Lanterns."

Response to Magic Lanterns was so positive among Ogilvy's clients and prospective clients that David decided this information had to be told to business leaders across America. Breaking from industry tradition, he launched a series of full-page advertisements in business newspapers explaining in black and white what his agency had discovered. These ads featured headlines like "How to launch new products," "How to create food advertising that sells," "How to advertise travel," and "How to make successful television commercials." The campaign brought in new clients, but more important, it added a luster to the Ogilvy brand in the eyes of many business movers and shakers. No ad agency in America had ever done anything like it before.

KNOW THE PRODUCT AND THE CLIENT

Ogilvy held the opinion that his agency's clients offered products to consumers that were of excellent value for the selling price. For him, using his clients' products on a daily basis was essential to understanding how to position these brands and create advertising campaigns that sell the product. His shirts were Hathaway, his crystal candlesticks Steuben, the car he drove was a Rolls-Royce, its tank was always filled with Super Shell. At breakfast, he took either Maxwell House Coffee or Tetley Tea and ate Pepperidge Farm toast. He washed with Dove soap, used Ban deodorant, and relied on a Zippo lighter. He drank Puerto Rico rum with Schweppes soda. His travel reservations were made through an American Express travel agency and he made an effort to fly on KLM or P&O-Orient Airlines.

In the early years it was easy for Ogilvy to work side-by-side with every employee. Communications and affections were not hard to cultivate and maintain. But as the staff grew into the hundreds (later into the thousands), he found it difficult to communicate with people he didn't know by first name or by sight.

So once a year, starting in 1954, he assembled all Ogilvy people in the auditorium of MoMA to give them a frank report on the agency's operations. He told them what he expected of them and the kind of behavior he admired in men and women. Qualities like working hard, biting the bullet, sharpening their brains, being self-confident, building up staff, having gentle manners, and treating other people like human beings. For people who knew and worked with Ogilvy, these were not platitudes scripted by a speech writer, they were his words spoken from the heart.

Ogilvy would then tell his people what he expected of himself. To be fair, yet firm. To keep the agency vital and to build it by landing new accounts. To win the confidence of Ogilvy's clients at the highest level. To be profitable to keep all of them, including himself, from penury in old age. To plan policies far into the future. To recruit only the brightest people. To be the hottest agency in the business, and to get the best out of every man and woman.

Ogilvy knew that his agency's success depended more than anything else on his ability to find people who could create great campaigns. He wanted people with "fire in their bellies."

When he noticed a great ad, he would find out who created it. Then he would call the copywriter to convey his praise for the exceptional work. The call often induced the person to ask if there was an opening at Ogilvy.

Ogilvy's determination to hire first-class people with smart brains is best conveyed in this story told to me by Jock Elliott. "I recall it vividly," he said. "It was at the board of directors meeting in the summer of 1962. David had not yet entered the room, but on the table in front of everyone was a small toy doll shaped like an egg (Elliott was referring to a Matrioshka doll from Gorky). The design was so constructed that it was apparent it was meant to be opened. As I did so, I found a small piece of paper that had been folded into the doll's body. Removing it from its housing, I proceeded to unfold it, and found this message: 'If each of us hires people who are smaller than we are, we will become a company of dwarfs. But if each of us hires people who are bigger than we are, we will become a company of giants.' David being David, made his point in the most graphic way possible. From that point on, he received the board's full cooperation in recruiting the brightest people."

Even today, when someone is appointed head of one of the agency's offices, Ogilvy & Mather's CEO and chairwoman Shelly Lazarus sends him a Matrioshka doll with the same message inside. So, the tradition continues on almost four decades later. Now that's WOW!

BECOMING AN INTERNATIONAL AGENCY

The year of 1964 marked a turning point for Ogilvy & Mather. It merged with Mather & Crowther to become an international agency with offices in London, Frankfurt, Vienna, and Milan. Then in 1971, Ogilvy London acquired S.H. Benson. The Benson agency gave Ogilvy more accounts and offices in Europe and in Southeast Asia.

With the merger, acquisition, and having become a publicly held company, David Ogilvy had become legendary in the ad business, and rightfully so. After all, he invented some of the most memorable brand icons in the annals of advertising history including the "Hathaway Man," recognized by his black eye patch; Commander Whitehead in ad campaigns for Schweppes; and Teddy Roosevelt's "Good to the last drop," which became a lasting brand slogan for Maxwell House coffee.

In 1973, Ogilvy made newspaper headlines with the announcement that he was leaving New York so that he and his wife could take up residency in a fourteenth century castle in France. Many in the ad business questioned his ability to remain an effective chief creative head of such a major agency working from the French countryside. And there were those in the trade press who predicted the eventual demise of Ogilvy & Mather without its brightest star.

Apparently, these were more of the outside world's perceptions than they were within the agency. The critics failed to see the organization—the creative talent and account management—that had been put in place under Ogilvy's direction since the late 1950s. The people in charge at Ogilvy knew that business would go forward as always. Why? Ogilvy taught them how to run an agency, and he put it all down in books—and he left it to all of them. Ogilvy had put together a first-class team of men and women capable of taking Ogilvy to heights that he never experienced during his reign over the agency. In 1975, Ogilvy retired from the agency he built, but he retained the title of worldwide creative head.

OGILVY'S BRAND SECRET

The primary ingredient that has built—and continues to build—the Ogilvy brand are the core principles that embody the beliefs of its founder. Remove this body of doctrines and the identity of its founder, David Ogilvy, and Ogilvy & Mather Worldwide will become another nondescript ad agency. What is significant here is not the content of the principles, per se, but why the principles have been kept alive. After all, the agency has carried on for more than a quarter of a century without David Ogilvy's active role in it. Perhaps the great ad man himself said it best, "In our business, people are hungry for dogma. Here there is a religion with all the little things and the big things—it's our style of management."

Throughout his career, Ogilvy observed that creative people want and need a religion—something to believe in and to work for. He also recognized that without a leader to identify with, these people often were restless and uncertain of their mission. Thus, beyond the sound business logic of many of Ogilvy's tenets, they actually serve a need that has a direct bearing on the quality of the creative work produced at the agency.

PURSUIT OF KNOWLEDGE

While many advertising executives hold the opinion that the differences between the best advertising agencies are small and usually perceived from the inside, the fact is, the differences are there. And perhaps what separates the Ogilvy agency from the pack is its pursuit of knowledge. "David Ogilvy always preached the simple idea that the more you know about what you're doing, the more likely you will do it well," commented Gray.

Ogilvy's CEO Shelly Lazarus remains infected with the idea of keeping David Ogilvy's teachings alive and vibrant. "When copywriters, art directors—everybody involved in the process of creating advertising—come to work at Ogilvy, they are taught David's insights on how to write headlines and body copy for print advertisements, and how to create TV commercials that capture the essence of the product in a genuine selling idea," said Lazarus.

Lazarus also sees to it that account executives joining Ogilvy are given intense training in the agency's art of management practices regardless of their professional background and prior agency training. "Some new recruits are uneasy at the notion of working within such rigid disciplines. They tend to argue that these 'road maps' will produce dull advertising," said Lazarus. "My reply is, 'It hasn't so far.'"

Keep in mind that Leonardo da Vinci religiously adhered to the established principles of "golden rectangular portions" used by Renaissance masters before him. That didn't stop him from creating masterpieces.

Ogilvy goes to great lengths to praise its people. In 1980, it established the Jules Fine Award for the individual at the agency displaying the highest standards of professionalism combined with civility. Who is Jules Fine, you ask?

He was Ogilvy's U.S. director of marketing services. "It's not easy to live up to the standard that Jules set in his work, and as a human being," said Gray. The first recipient of the Jules Fine Award was librarian Joanne Winiarski in 1981. Her prize was an all-expense-paid trip to anywhere for two.

THINK AND ACT LIKE A SMALLER AGENCY

"I've often thought about Jay Chiat's famous question, 'How big can an agency become before it becomes bad?' The answer is there is no limit—so long as you continue to think and act like a small agency," said Boyko in a recent *Wall Street Journal* advertisement. Ogilvy wanted to build a big-league agency from the day he opened his shop. But he also knew that his agency's best creative work was when it was small and hungry—willing to go out on a limb to find a big campaign idea. Thinking and acting like a small agency is one of the challenges every creative chief at Ogilvy has to face on a daily basis. "At Ogilvy, we're focused on nurturing an entrepreneurial spirit, keeping a flat structure with a minimum of hierarchy and layers, and relying on an open environment where anyone has a chance to express ideas and communicate freely and without fear," remarked Boyko.

Using every yardstick to measure the success of an ad agency, Ogilvy has come out on top or near the top in every category. Yet despite its success and fast growth rate, it has not forgotten how it got there—and the principles it must preserve and nurture.

Unlike many other corporations, each generation of management has had the wisdom to recognize and value the many qualities that comprise the agency's brand personality. Further, management has made, through example, many disciples of the Ogilvy religion in all departments of the agency to insure continuation of the brand's integrity in the decades to come.

Perhaps these words spoken by CEO Shelly Lazarus to Ogilvy & Mather Worldwide employees sums up best what can be gained for every company by keeping the person's name on the business door who represents the company's distinctive values and vision: "The use of David's own signature as a brand icon makes a strong, personal and yet contemporary connection to David, and it does so in every office, for every discipline. More than any typographical rendering could, David's handwritten name offers value beyond the graphics—it is bold, elegant, evocative, human, timeless, and uniquely ours. Coupled with Ogilvy Red, it is also dramatic and distinctive. Used together, their sum is greater than the parts."

LESSONS LEARNED

1. One of the most effective ways to build a company's flagship brand is to make its founder a hero in the minds of consumers, employees, shareholders, and others. KFC's Colonel Sanders, Wendy's Dave Thomas, Amazon.com's Jeff Bezos, and Apple's Steve Jobs are examples.

2. Never lose sight of the core principles put down in writing by your company's founder unless you want to follow in the footsteps of F.W. Woolworth.

3. No matter how big your company becomes, think and act like a smaller company that is willing to take risks to achieve brand marketing WOW.

4. Contrary to what you've heard or read, adhering to proven principles is the springboard to creative expression that hits brand slams.

5. Hire the brightest people in your industry if you want to become a company of giants.

6. Come up with a genuine selling idea for a new product or service experience and you've loaded the bases for a chance to hit a brand slam campaign—all it takes is a brilliant execution of that idea to blow away your competition.

18

HERMAN MILLER RAISES THE STANDARD FOR PRODUCT EXCELLENCE

"Once you've surpassed mediocrity, you lose the right to return to it."

Charles Eames

In 1979, I purchased a summer home on Bainbridge Island, a thirty-minute ferry ride across Puget Sound to downtown Seattle. I had some furniture items including three Herman Miller Ergon work chairs, which I had purchased from a Los Angeles dealer in 1975, delivered from my office near Beverly Hills. A few months later, the swivel mechanism on two of the chairs made an odd clicking sound when the seats were turned. I called Herman Miller's customer service department in Michigan to find out if there was someone in the Seattle area who could repair the chairs. I wasn't expecting Herman Miller to make good on the repair cost since the chairs were five years old.

The company's representative told me that Herman Miller would take care of the problem. "You'll be hearing from an authorized service technician in forty-eight hours," she said. Her words were like music to my ears, but I didn't believe her. No customer service representatives return phone calls.

But sure enough, two days later, a service technician called for directions to my home. He told me that he was flying in from San Francisco and renting a car at the airport. "We don't have a service technician experienced in changing your chair's swivel mechanism in the Seattle area," he said.

"This is too good to be true," I said to myself. The next day he rang my doorbell. Within an hour, the two chairs were as good as new, and I

thanked him for a job well done. Herman Miller's cost to bring this technician from San Francisco to my home had to be more than the price I paid
for the two chairs.

The fact that Herman Miller stepped up to the plate and assumed responsibility for its product's integrity hit me with considerable impact. I was
convinced that this company's outstanding after-sales service had to be told
in print. I contacted the company's then communications director and told
him of my interest in writing a story about Herman Miller for a business
publication. He was very receptive to the idea and graciously extended to
me an invitation to visit the company's headquarters in Zeeland, Michigan.
He then informed me that I would be staying at the company's Marigold
Lodge.

About two weeks later, a chauffeured car was waiting for me at the
Grand Rapids airport to take me to the Marigold Lodge in Holland, Michigan. Nearby the site of the company's headquarters, I recall the driver
telling me that Zeeland was a small community with 4,000 residents,
twenty churches, and no bars. At that time, alcoholic beverages weren't
served at Marigold. "Well, Zeeland may be the only place in America where
Frank Sinatra and his Rat Pack would turn down a gig," I said. He laughed.

What stands out most in my mind was the interview I had with Herman Miller's then chairman and CEO, Max DePree. A soft-spoken man, he
impressed me with his philosophical approach to running a big manufacturing company. While DePree had much wealth, he was diametrical in
style from the flamboyant Lee Iacoccas out there. He was definitely in the
Warren Buffet genre, preferring to remain out of the limelight.

After meeting with other top executives, I was given a tour of the company's manufacturing facility. The next day, I attended a few work team
meetings. That evening, I met with the renowned industrial designer
George Nelson. Nelson, whom I took to be in his seventies at that time,
told me how he singlehandedly catapulted Herman Miller into the big-
leagues via his furniture design creations of the 1950s. Being able to deal
with the egos of designers like Nelson was another one of DePree's gifts.

DePree then made a statement, which I wrote down in my notebook
under the heading "unforgettable thoughts by prominent business leaders."
He said, "You must have a strong point of view and believe in your gut feeling. Don't lead people, but inspire them by your own actions to follow
you."

The name Herman Miller has long been synonymous with the design
and manufacture of classic furniture like the Eames lounge chair and ottoman. Today, it is best known for the manufacturing and sale of innovative
chairs like the Aeron and office systems products and related services.

Herman Miller's business philosophy fosters creativity and excellence.
Its ability to produce high-quality products extends to the outer aspects of
its brand's identity. That is, what its customers see is a reflection of what the

company is. The company is as well-known around the world as industrial giants ten times its size. Like other companies featured in *Brand Slam,* Herman Miller does "first-class business in a first-class way."

For almost eight decades, Herman Miller has not only pioneered furniture and office systems design, but human relations, too. The company's founder, D.J. DePree, said, "A business is rightfully judged by its products and services, but it must also face scrutiny and judgment as to its humanity." DePree's golden rules of doing business, set down in writing by him, have influenced every CEO who has been at the helm, including the present one, Mike Volkema.

The DePrees, who ran the company for most of the past century are remembered by long-time employees and retirees as being gentle, soft-spoken, and respectful people. They regarded everyone who worked for Herman Miller as family. That thinking continues on today under CEO Volkema's watch. What might be considered old-fashioned virtues are much in evidence in the company's brand culture. Top executives often refer to their "stewardship" of products and the company's "covenant" with employees. They expect honesty from all of their employees. At the same time, they recognize that the office systems industry is highly competitive. They believe business survival is their greatest responsibility to their employees and shareholders.

With the strength of new products coming to market, coupled with its investments in enterprise technology, CEO Volkema sees the potential to create dramatic new value for customers and shareholders. Net sales were $1.94 billion for the fiscal year ending June 31, 2000, compared with net sales of $1.76 billion in the prior year. Today, one-third of all businesses use what is now referred to as open-plan offices. Herman Miller is the leader in the industry with more than 1 million individuals using its office systems products worldwide.

Along with financial success, the company has gathered other kinds of recognition. Here are three recent examples: In 1998, *Fortune* magazine noted Herman Miller as the "Most Admired Company in America for Social Responsibility." The prior year, the same magazine recognized Herman Miller among the "100 Best Companies to Work for in America." In 1998, *Industry Week* magazine cited Herman Miller as one of the world's "100 Best-Managed Manufacturers."

A number of Herman Miller's designs are in the permanent collections of major museums, including New York's Museum of Modern Art and the Whitney Museum, the Smithsonian Institute in Washington, D.C., and in other design collections around the world. Herman Miller attracts the brightest industrial designers in the world to partner with the company to produce innovative products and office systems designs.

When you look into this company's history, you see that people are what Herman Miller is most committed to—employees, outside designers and architects, customers, and shareholders. "People are the heart and spirit of all we deal with," said Volkema. "It is a commitment of ownership and one that directly leads to the concept of legacy. When we talk about a legacy in this sense, we are talking about the roots of the corporation, about the sense of continuity, about the corporate culture. To what do the owners of a company commit, and what do they wish to leave to their corporate heirs?"

DESIGN TAKES CENTER STAGE

The Herman Miller Company was established in 1923, when D.J. DePree took over the Michigan Star Furniture factory where he had worked for fourteen years. He renamed the company in honor of his wife's father, who helped finance the deal. During the 1920s, the firm progressed in a modest way, introducing new standards of quality for case goods including furniture, bookcases, and bureaus that provided interior storage. These were sold by such retailers as Sears, Roebuck & Company.

By the summer of 1930, D.J. DePree was looking for a new niche in an eroding market. He was, therefore, eager to meet industrial designer Gilbert Rohde. While DePree knew practically nothing about design, designers, or the design process, he had the insight to see the diversity of gifts in people. This enabled him to accept outside designers like Rohde and others who would follow. But most of all, he listened to them and allowed them to exercise their talents.

During the 1930s and early 1940s, the company faced the tough transition from making good quality, traditional copies of furniture to learning how to sell Rohde's new modern furniture. By the mid-forties, D.J. DePree hired George Nelson as outside design director and was again back in the vanguard of "design-for-living" concepts.

Nelson contributed to Herman Miller a broad range of designs including the Sling Sofa, the L-Shaped Desk, the Comprehensive Storage System, and the company's logo. Nelson's magnetism and reputation attracted top designers and architects to Herman Miller. Chief among them were Alexander Girard, one of the great colorists and pattern creators; and Charles Eames, called the most original American furniture designer since Duncan Phyfe.

Eames' first brand slam product for Herman Miller was a version of the molded plywood chair for which he, in collaboration with famed architect Eero Saarinen, had won the Museum of Modern Art's "Organic Design in Home Furnishings" competition. More molded chairs and seating for offices and airports were designed by Eames for Herman Miller's collection. The molded plywood Eames lounge chair was named "Design of the Century" by *Time* magazine in its final edition of the twentieth century.

The DePrees learned much from Eames about achieving WOW in furniture design and the importance of leadership. He helped management understand its role as a problem solver, to analyze situations, and to develop innovative solutions to the problems it uncovered. He reinforced the concept of excellence in all things that D.J. DePree had fostered decades earlier.

BRAND SLAM PRODUCT BECOMES AMERICAN ICON

When a company hits a brand slam with an innovative product that defines its time, that product is forever etched in the minds of consumers. For Herman Miller, its most recognized brand slam product through most of the twentieth century was the Eames lounge chair and ottoman introduced in 1956. Made of wood veneer and supple leather, this chair and ottoman appear in residences and offices all over the world. The original Eames lounge chair and ottoman, now considered by many leading museums to be an American furniture icon of the twentieth century, continues to be produced by Herman Miller in the twenty-first century.

While sales of this product are dwarfed by office systems products, Herman Miller has been known to spend money to restore this classic lounge chair and ottoman for customers who purchased the set in the late 1950s. How many manufacturers have such an affinity for the products that bear their brand's name?

A COMPANY THAT RENEWS ITSELF

Innovative products often appear to outsiders as the single ingredient that has made Herman Miller successful. But within the organization, people will tell you it is openness to change that contributed most to the company's success.

To remain innovative and continue to be an industry leader, a company must value the benefits of renewal. D.J. DePree had already learned this through his experiences with Rohde, Nelson, Eames, and others who had helped Herman Miller constantly sharpen its understanding of itself. DePree's experiences had shown that a climate of trust and openness allowed for creativity, leadership, and genius to emerge. Because he believed every person to be unique, he believed that such a climate should be nurtured, both because it ought to be and because it made good business sense.

This thinking was further impressed upon the firm's executives by Dr. Carl Frost, a behavioral psychologist who agreed to work with D.J. DePree in 1949, to help the company increase productivity. Frost convinced De-Pree to adopt the Scanlon Plan, which led to the development of a collaborative relationship between management and factory workers. The plan is based on principles of identity, participation, accountability, managerial competency, and equity. DePree saw the need to enlist the support of all employees to reduce delivery times and to raise product workmanship to the level of design quality.

Managing such participation of employees is simply a way to help reduce the odds of failure when having to manage conflict or change. "It's not an easy way to manage. Yet, Herman Miller has shown that greater achievement results when sound principles of cooperative employee relations are at work," said Volkema.

The Scanlon principles have stood the test of time. Max DePree once said, "The first step of leadership is to define reality. The last step is to say thank you to those who got the job done. Everything else is in between."

Under the plan, employees gain a return on their contribution from monthly bonuses based upon performance that meets or exceeds productivity goals. The bonus calculation considers all employees' contributions in cost savings, in service to the customer, and in the management of human resources, material, and money.

Through the years, management has always held the belief that every employee should be involved in the running of the business. That still remains true today. All managers or supervisors, called "work team leaders," include members of their team in decision making where and when appropriate. "All of our employee-owners have something to contribute to a particular management decision that could improve work performance and profits," remarked Volkema.

With competitors entering its markets in the early 1980s with alternative open-plan office systems, the need to become innovative at the dealer level was obvious to Max DePree. So, management developed a participatory relationship with its dealers. This worked well and helped Herman Miller to maintain its position as the leader in its industry.

Herman Miller's management takes every opportunity to remind its employees and shareholders of the company's heritage, culture, and the products that catapulted the Herman Miller brand to global marketing stardom. These reminders in speeches, annual reports, brochures, posters, company newspapers, and on its Web site convey to employees that they are a part of something much larger than themselves.

How many CEOs today would start their company's home page with an historical statement from their company's founder? Herman Miller's Volkema did just that. It brings to mind the New York Yankees who have won twenty-six World Series championships, more than any other baseball franchise. Visit Yankee Stadium in the Bronx, New York, and you'll find bronze statues or plaques of its heroes including Babe Ruth, Lou Gehrig, Joe DiMaggio, and Mickey Mantle. Every six-year-old Yankee fan is told about the great ones who put on the pinstripes.

FINDING PROFIT CENTERS

At Herman Miller, the word *research* means the ability to identify customer needs and then to develop solutions to satisfy those needs. It was Herman Miller's researcher Robert Propst who in the 1960s developed the open-plan office landscape system, which he named "Action Office." Propst's big idea at that time gave birth to a new industry segment. The orders for office systems products are now in the billions of dollars. Now that's WOW!

Propst's system called for replacing fixed interior walls with moveable partitions of various heights. These partitions, offering some degree of privacy, supported height-adjustable desks, storage units, and other pieces to accommodate office equipment, telephones, and PCs. The idea was to design each work space within a facility to fit the kind of work being done, and to boost productivity as well.

PARTNERING WITH OUTSIDE DESIGNERS

Herman Miller has partnered with and nurtured outside industrial designers and architects including Isamu Noguchi, Bruce Burdick, Clino Castelli, Bill Stumpf, Wolfgang Mueller-Deisig, and Jorgen Rasmussen. One of its newest partners is Turkish-born Ayse Birsel, considered by Herman Miller to be one of the hottest industrial designers in the world. The company gives outside designers advances against royalties, much like a book publisher. The royalties on sales have motivated these designers to push the new product's envelope.

This ongoing investment in innovative product design is clear evidence of CEO Volkema's belief that the workplace will never be without problems awaiting solutions. "Because people are different and because office work constantly changes, only those manufacturers able to respond quickly with the best solutions will thrive," said Volkema. "While the future growth of Herman Miller is expected to come largely from its open-plan systems, new concepts of seating and holding objects used in the workplace will find their way to the market, too."

Back in 1976, Herman Miller hit brand slams with Stumpf's Ergon office chairs, and again in 1984 with Stumpf's equally innovative Equa chairs. Both products applied new technology in response to people with differing physiques and job functions who require different seating support, while in search of ergonomic seating comfort.

When the Burdick Group was launched in the mid-1980s, it had WOW power for corporate executives looking for breakthrough office furniture design. It features work-support tools such as paper organizers, electronic-machine supports, and work surfaces that attach quickly and easily to a horizontal beam. The beam-constructed desk allows executives to tailor their workplaces to suit their particular tasks.

The commitment to design excellence and innovation is a trademark of Herman Miller. This legacy remains in large part due to the inspiration of the DePrees and other design leaders including Nelson and the Eameses who prepared the way for Volkema and his management team.

The point is that outside designers are free to explore concepts without Herman Miller's management looking over their shoulders. When designers believe they have developed a product with a big idea, they can take it to a working prototype. It is then presented to management for possible suggestions for modification or revision. This same freedom is given to all people providing a creative function whether it be in advertising, print graphics, or Web design construction.

Why so much creative freedom? Management has learned that trust in outside designers, like trust in employees, is often repaid tenfold. "Solving problems through innovation could not be done without strong relations with our outside designers and the company's commitment to product excellence," said Gary Miller, executive vice president of product development and research.

Graphics and Facilities That Say WOW

Creativity is what makes Herman Miller's print advertising and promotional items better than those of industrialists ten times its size. Annual reports, product brochures, and posters are highly imaginative.

Through graphics, Herman Miller has shown the business world that a manufacturer of office systems products can produce joyful and spontaneous shapes, colors, illustrations, and human themes. For example, the company's graphics in the 1970s and 1980s under the direction of Stephen Fykholm are standouts. The Fykholm series of posters for Herman Miller's annual summer picnics captured the spirit of these events while racking up gold awards from the American Institute of Graphic Arts, and all major New York advertising shows. Today, they are much sought-after poster art for residences and offices. They also reside in the New York Museum of Modern Art's permanent collection.

The company conveys its dedication to design excellence in the exemplary quality of its award-winning architecture in its showrooms, offices, and manufacturing plants around the world. Taking such an interest in the selling environment is not new to Herman Miller. While the manufacturer's furniture showroom is commonplace today, it wasn't so in the 1930s. D.J. DePree believed innovations like Rohde's modern furniture required equally innovative merchandising and he set out to make it happen. The result was the opening of the Herman Miller showroom in Chicago in 1939.

Today, Herman Miller showrooms play a major role in introducing thousands of people to the company and its product lines. Its classy-looking showrooms, designed by the company's interiors group, usually have a large presentation room, along with open areas for special events.

When Herman Miller builds a new manufacturing facility, management is thinking about the people who will be working there. Its Holland, Michigan, "Greenhouse" facility serves as a showcase for its products. The building features a system of windows, as well as skylights that ensure every worker of being within 100 feet of a source of natural light.

When it comes to presenting its brand's personality through its facilities, however, the Marigold Lodge near Lake Michigan, formerly a private summer retreat for a Chicago industrialist, says it all. It clearly shows the high value Herman Miller puts upon excellence and quality, upon preserving the best of the past, and its concern both for people and things. "Marigold Lodge has to do with civility. That's why we wanted it," said Max DePree.

Originally designed by the Chicago firm of Tallmage and Watson in 1913, the spacious prairie style house was purchased by Herman Miller in 1978. After undertaking an ambitious renovation and restoration program, the lodge became the corporate hospitality center. The grounds also include a conference and learning center. Marigold is a skillful blend of the old and new. As such, it demonstrates to guests (mostly customers) that Herman Miller's modern furniture works well in traditional settings, too. "Good architecture is not an effort to show off to people that we understand architecture. It's an effort to put people into the right kind of working environment," noted Volkema.

The people at Herman Miller are not into strategies, strategies, and more strategies. They bring to the ball game people with vision, guts, determination, and talent. And these people have demonstrated their ability to knock the ball out of the park with the bases loaded.

But when you look at this company's exceptional record of hitting so many brand slam products, one thing stands out: Herman Miller has taken charge of the elements that comprise its brand's identity. It knows what it wants that brand to be and how to back it up with the products it chooses to manufacture and market.

Its relentless pursuit of product excellence and adherence to time-tested principles of doing business have paid off big time for its shareholders. A mere $1,000 invested in Herman Miller (MLHR on the Nasdaq) stock when it first went public on September 24, 1970, would now be worth $101,420 as of June 2, 2000. That's over 100 times the original investment and over 5.6 times the performance of the Standard & Poor index during the same period.

LESSONS LEARNED

1. Focus on customer needs in search of new products and services that provide real solutions to those needs.

2. Partner with outside people who are considered geniuses in their industry and give them total freedom to exercise their gifts. Motivate them to achieve excellence by giving them royalties on the sales of the product they invent or design that you manufacture and bring to market.

3. Make your people look like heroes to your customers, Wall Street, and the media. Your company will be rewarded tenfold.

4. If a new product idea looks, sounds, and smells like mediocrity, then move on to something else.

5. To grow and prosper, every employee must be encouraged to embrace the values inherent within the company's brand culture, and to support those interdependent individuals responsible for developing breakaway products and services.

19

EMERIL LAGASSE'S OUTRAGEOUS ENTHUSIASM SCORES A BRAND SLAM

Behind every powerhouse brand you'll find a powerhouse celebrity or a beloved icon. Emeril Lagasse is that brand celebrity, and right now he's the hottest chef on the planet. His outrageous sense of humor, like the way he yells "bam!" when he tosses in the ingredients, has made him a national icon.

OK, so now you're asking, "What am I going to learn from a TV celebrity chef about hitting a brand slam for my company's products?" First, you'll learn that all-out enthusiasm about your company's products or services is absolutely contagious, no matter what industry you're in.

Second, you'll learn that when you express your passion for the products your company makes, you're making powerful human contact. And that's what creates WOW in the minds of consumers. Third, you'll learn that credibility with your audience is key to climbing the ladder of brand success. Finally, you'll learn that it takes improvisation and reinvention, not just strategies to keep your brand on top.

JOURNEY TO THE TOP

While most boys his age were playing baseball in sand lots, Emeril Lagasse was working at a Portuguese bakery in his Fall River, Massachusetts, neighborhood. It was here that he would learn the art of bread and pastry making. Years later when he was offered a music scholarship, he turned it down to pursue his dream of becoming a world-class chef. He worked his way through the Johnson and Wales University culinary program, earning a Doctorate degree.

With a focus on classic French cuisine, Emeril went off to Paris and Lyons to polish his culinary skills. Returning to the United States, he worked in several fine restaurants in New York, Boston, and Philadelphia. Soon word got around about this talented young chef's passion for his craft coupled with his insistence on using only the finest, freshest ingredients. Ella Brennan, considered to be the doyenne of New Orleans' culinary world persuaded the then twenty-six-year-old chef Lagasse to move to the Big Easy to take charge of her and Dick Brennan's famous restaurant, Commander's Palace.

After a seven-and-a-half year stint at Brennan's, where he received enormous critical acclaim, Lagasse opened Emeril's Restaurant in 1990. And the man known for reinventing every meal drew high praise from the local New Orleans gentry, the food writers at *Esquire, Conde Nast Traveler,* and *Travel & Leisure,* as well as from noted food critics John Mariani and Gene Bourg. He went on to open five more successful restaurants and soon became the host of two popular cable TV shows. Yet, with such meteoric success, his friends and the people who know him best say he hasn't changed much. He remains devoted as ever to his craft and is always inventing new cuisine.

A HOUSEHOLD NAME

It's no wonder that Emeril Lagasse has become a national icon. The faces of Lagasse and fellow celebrity chefs Wolfgang Puck, and Julia Child are more familiar to Americans than the faces of most U.S. senators. Still, Lagasse—more commonly known as simply, Emeril—has some heavy competition.

Take Julia Child, for example. Four decades ago she was the first chef to have her own TV cooking show on a national network. While each cast member of NBC's hit TV show *Friends* will receive $800,000 per episode over the next two years, Child received a whopping $50 for each episode she appeared in back then. Her peers have called her an American cultural icon and the empress of American cooking. Whether she's cooking a classic French dish or a hamburger, her passion for food never stops. The success of her first book on French cuisine created a new category segment in book publishing. She went on to author a dozen more best-selling cookbooks. If you think it's too late to start a new career, consider that Child didn't take a cooking lesson until she was thirty-seven.

Another celebrity chef, Martin Yan has authored twenty-two books on Chinese and Asian cooking. He sees himself more as a teaching chef, then a celebrity chef. No one cuts, chops, dices, or talks faster than Yan. He makes wok stir-fried cooking look simple and easy. Creating colorful and appetizing Asian-inspired dishes is what built the Martin Yan brand.

Food Network's *Too Hot Tamales* TV show chefs Mary Sue Milliken and Susan Feniger are partners in the successful Border Grill restaurants in Santa Monica and Las Vegas and the restaurant Cludad in Los Angeles. While they cook up ethnic dishes from around the world on their popular cable show, the chefs have become known, says *New York Newsday,* as Mexican food's "preeminent American translators." You get the feeling they started cooking together when they were Girl Scouts.

Bobby Flay is also a well-known "TV chef." He is good-looking, talkative, easy going, and funny. He prefers casual clothes over the traditional chef's whites and is never seen wearing an apron. The flirtatious and attractive Jacqui Malouf is Flay's sidekick on the *Hot Off the Grill With Bobby Flay* show on Food Network. Even though she leaves all of the "real" cooking to Flay, she's still "cooking" for men in the twenty-five to forty-five age group. As Regis Philbin once said, "Some TV shows need to be co-hosted by a man and a woman to keep the conversation interesting." The show's set is reminiscent of a New York Soho loft. Fans, seated on sofas or chairs, wait patiently to dig into Flay's off-the-grill creations and to sample a wine or beer that enhances the main dish served. Flay, who's into mild to medium-hot chilies, owns a popular New York City restaurant known for Southwestern cuisine.

Making Italian cooking look simple and showing a passion for cooking belongs to TV chef Mario Batali. The *Molto Mario* Food Network show reaches 45 million people around the world. Batali lived three years in Italy studying the secrets of regional and local cooking. Whatever Batali cooks, it's from the heart.

Graham Kerr, known to millions as "The Galloping Gourmet," earned the title of the most popular TV chef in 1969. His light-of-heart style of cooking masks the fact that he is probably the most experienced chef among his peers in the business of TV cooking shows. In 1971, Kerr and his TV producer wife were almost killed in a serious automobile accident. After three years and 300 episodes, *The Galloping Gourmet* TV series came to an end. Today, a much older Kerr with a slower gallop in his stride has his own show on the cable Food Network called *Graham Kerr's Gathering Place.* Once known for a chef catering to gastronomic excessiveness, Kerr is now whipping up lighter food dishes that he says are good for your health. More than 10 million copies of Kerr's twenty-three cookbooks are in print. Now that's WOW!

Wolfgang Puck is a story of rags to riches. This Austrian-born chef with a thick German accent made his name as the chef for Ma Maison and later as the owner and head chef of Spago in Los Angeles. Spago, by the way, is Italian slang for pasta. Puck was the first to turn a restaurant's kitchen into a stage performance. Today, he and his wife own several hot restaurants all over the country. Puck is known for making celebrities including Johnny Carson and the late Walter Matheau feel right at home at any one of his eateries. According to *Fortune,* Puck is the wealthiest chef in America, earning $10 million annually. Part of that income comes from the sales of Wolfgang Puck's frozen gourmet pizzas. The official chef at the annual Academy Awards, Puck has been known to fly in from all over the country 200 or more chefs to produce his seven-course Oscar dishes.

While all of these chefs are masters of the culinary arts, and all of them have creative WOW, none seem to match the outrageous enthusiasm that chef Emeril Lagasse has for food and his craft.

Much the same way that Michael Jordan dominated the basketball court, no one is going to upstage Emeril on TV cooking shows. In fact, he often says to his viewers, "Hey, they don't cook food like this in those other studios." His critics say he's too loud and wild or that he makes a mockery of culinary arts by yelling "Bam!" as he throws a hefty pinch of his essence spice onto his finished creation. Then there are those health dietitians who say his public proclamation that "Pork fat rules baby!" is only adding to the obesity problem in America.

Yet, Emeril's fans love his excessiveness and bold style of cooking. "You like garlic in your Cajun chicken? Well, I'm adding forty-four cloves to mine!" he blares out to a cheering live studio audience. Emeril helps people to remember what *real cooking* and *real food* are all about. When he makes a sauce with butter or mayonnaise, he's not thinking about calories or saturated fat. *Emeril Live* is not for the faint-hearted or those hooked on Stouffer's Lean Cuisine or Weight Watchers' Smart Ones frozen meals.

Emeril's restaurants exhibit the same flair. As of June 2000, he has six signature restaurants including Emeril's Restaurant, and Nola and Delmonico's, both in New Orleans; Emeril's New Orleans Fish House and Emeril's Delmonico Steakhouse in Las Vegas; and Emeril's Restaurant Orlando at Universal Studios Escape. The latter is ranked among the best restaurants in the world. The entire staff spent six weeks in training for opening day. Some 17,000 bottles of wine can be viewed in state-of-the-art climate control wall-to-wall storage units. The kitchen design and equipment are unmatched by any restaurant.

On Emeril's Web site (www.emerils.com) you'll find "Get Cool Stuff Here, Baby!" Believe me, this chef is doing more than just planning the meals for his TV show. Unlike his competitors, the brand "Emeril" goes beyond the chef's signature dishes and cookbooks. There's Emerilware, gift certificates, coffee, spices, T-shirts, baseplates, a music CD, baseball caps, polo shirts, and chef coats all emblazoned with the Emeril trademark. Then there's the planned Emeril's Cooking Club for kids. Who knows, perhaps an Emeril cologne for men is just around the corner.

AN EMERIL'S HOME STORE?

On a grander scale, I can envision an "Emeril's Home Store" in every big city in the world. Wouldn't that get the attention of Crate & Barrel's management! The array of products that could be sold under Emeril's brand is mind-boggling—New Orleans-inspired furniture, area rugs, window curtains, pantry cabinets, flatware, bedding, bathrobes, towels, glasses, candles, planting pots, outdoor swings, and just about everything else for home living that speaks to "the best of Emeril" in quality products. The brand "Emeril" has earned what I call a *free agent* status. By that I mean, it's capable of being marketed on a broad range of products that bear no resemblance to the gourmet delicacies that put chef Emeril on the international map.

What I am proposing here is not "pie-in-the-sky dreaming." Emeril's Home Store could be company-owned, or it could be organized under a franchise system. Either way, the stores would kick up the Emeril brand to notches unknown to any TV celebrity chef.

Announcements on major TV news networks of a planned international chain of Emeril's retail stores would open doors for cobranding and licensing agreements with the biggest manufacturers around the world. Manufacturers today are looking to market their products under a powerhouse brand, and Emeril's brand certainly meets that criterion. The key is to enter into licensing agreements with manufacturers who pledge in writing not to alter or change the approved product's design, workmanship, and materials to cut manufacturing costs. Calvin Klein was recently in a billion-dollar lawsuit with the manufactuer of its world famous denim jeans. The designer Calvin Klein was on CNN's *Larry King Live* show in May 2000. He told the world that he was disappointed with the quality of denim used by the manuacturer licensed to make Calvin Klein branded jeans. King pointed out that now that Klein had said that on the show, people may not go out tomorrow and buy Calvin Klein denim jeans.

Klein agreed but suggested that what was at stake was the integrity of the Calvin Klein brand, and that that goes beyond money. There are a hundred different grades of denim and people who buy Calvin Klein jeans deserve to get the product that lives up to the brand's image.

THOSE MEMORABLE ONE LINERS

Emeril is known to his fans for his Portuguese Kale soup, roasted chicken stuffed with Chorizo sausage, and truffles with pasta. But he may be better known to them for his self-invented one-liners. The *Emeril Live* show's audience and millions of TV viewers get a charge out of hearing these hilarious comments from America's most popular chef. Here's the way Emeril talks:

"Kickin' it up to notches unknown, baby!" "Get to know your bird!" "Happy. Happy. Happy." "We aren't building rocket ships here!" "Who made these rules?" "It's food of love, baby!" "They've got lunatics across the street, we've got food!" "I don't know where you buy your flour, but mine doesn't come seasoned!" And of course, "bam!"

Memorable catchphrases and one-liners add to a brand's recognition factor. One of the great cinematic achievements, *Gone With the Wind* has its unforgettable one-liner: "Quite frankly, my dear, I don't give a damn!" Of course, Rhett Butler (played by Clark Gable) said it to Scarlett O'Hara (played by Vivien Leigh). In 1939, producer David O. Selznick pushed the envelope to the edge by allowing Gable to say the word "damn" on the silver screen. Hollywood screen writers have "come a long way, baby" since then.

According to comedian Jay Leno, the funniest one-liner of all time goes to Bill Clinton who, pointing his finger at the American people on national television, said, "I never had sex with that woman." Of course, he meant Monica Lewinski. Oops!

Emeril's one-liners are so memorable that his fans can recite them word for word. Yet, they probably couldn't tell you the ingredients he used in last night's show to prepare a Louisiana Creole dish.

These one-liners take the place of product slogans. They've helped etch the Emeril brand into the minds of millions of people. It's a mystery to me why other celebrity chefs haven't followed suit. Once again, the edge goes to Emeril Lagasse for building brand recognition.

Success Is in the Packaging

When I talk about the packaging of the Emeril brand, it goes far beyond chef Emeril Lagasse's skills, knowledge, and experience in cooking foods in front of TV cameras and a live studio audience. Let me switch to the automotive industry to make my point. There's only one Volkswagen New Beetle, only one Chrysler PT Cruiser, and only one Chevy Corvette—there are no other products like them that you can buy from a competing carmaker. When you're talking about food, however, that's not always the case. Any master chef can duplicate another master chef's signature dish by simply watching him or her make that dish on television and using the same quality of ingredients. Celebrity chefs give away their intellectual property rights to the product they've invented by publishing their recipe or talking about it on TV. Meanwhile, the original recipe for Coke syrup has been kept in an Atlanta Bank's vault since the late nineteenth century.

To get to the top rung of the ladder as fast as Emeril has done, required a masterful orchestration of his brand. In short, a lot has to do with the brand's total packaging. Here are some key elements of that packaging:

Studio Set Design

The producers of *Emeril Live* deserve much credit for the show's impressive set design. "Didn't they tell you that these were the dangerous seats?" asks Emeril to the people seated around the curved restaurant-like counter where the master chef cooks up his mouth-watering dishes. Of course, they and others seated at dining tables get to sample his finished products. And in typical Emeril style, he hands out extra forks to these folks and says, "Make some friends." If the theme of one night's show happens to be cooking with lobster, a large display of lobsters and other ingredients used in his dishes are attractively displayed along the counter's top. Live improvisational music comes into play before and after each commercial break. "Hey, give a hand to Doc Gibbs and Cliff," shouts Emeril to his studio audience. No other celebrity chef does that on cable TV. Once more, the advantage goes to Emeril Lagasse and the show's producers for brand-building smarts.

Attention-Getting Graphics

Graphics are an important element in the packaging of the Emeril brand; this is one more area in which Emeril stands out from his competitors. The exaggerated and distinctive letter "E" in the Emeril logo reflects this chef's love for his craft, his upbeat tempo, stylish attitude, and his "kick it up a notch" Louisiana-inspired dishes. No matter what the angle, every time the TV cameras scan the *Emeril Live* sound set, viewers see the "E" symbol displayed in various graphic treatments on the studio's walls and floor.

Each logo for Emeril's six restaurants captures the essence, uniqueness, or spirit of that restaurant's food theme, too. For example, when Emeril reopened the classic Delmonico's in New Orleans in 1998, he went with a big "D" cattle brand mark to capture the essence of a great steakhouse.

A Fun Web Site

Emerils.com is a fun place to visit and shop online. You'll find a smorgasbord of information about food news. There's recipes, topics on entertaining, feature articles about Emeril's restaurants, and upcoming events. Click on "The Market" and you'll see Emeril's gift ideas.

MASTER CHEF: KING OF IMPROVISATION

"Hey, I'm Emeril Lagasse, and we're here live in New York ready to cook up some incredible New Orleans dishes," shouts Emeril to his TV audience. "OK, I'm adding some good virgin olive oil to a hot pan . . . I love chorizo sausage, so I'm adding lots of it chopped up, if you don't like lots of it, add less . . . Can you smell the love that's happening right now, the fusion of the chorizo sausage flavors with the hot oil? . . . Next, I'm adding chopped onions, celery, and green bell peppers . . . Hey, if you like onions, add some more like I'm doing now . . . If you like garlic like I do, add as much as you like, I'm adding twenty-two chopped cloves to mine . . . Next, I'm adding some beautiful ripe red tomatoes that I chopped up earlier, not those orange-looking things you see in the supermarkets. . . ."

In another segment on *Emeril Live,* Emeril reinvents a classic gazpacho cold soup by adding English cucumber and lots of jicama. "Hey," he says, "I don't know about you, but I like Vodka in my gazpacho." He pours in some Absolut vodka, only the No. 1 brand, of course. "In fact," he adds, "I think I'll add more to kick it up a notch." He pours in more Absolut as the live audience cheers him on.

Well, I think you get my point that Emeril could not care less about adhering to a pre-scripted food segment. He's going to improvise and reinvent the dish he's making according to where his mind happens to be at that particular moment, and that is what his fans have come to expect from this talented chef.

Lessons Learned

1. Expressing outrageous enthusiasm about your company's products to consumers is your best sales pitch.

2. When you communicate your passion for the brands your company makes, you're making powerful human contact.

3. Never forget the power that a memorable one-liner can have with consumers.

4. A lot of what goes into building a powerhouse brand depends on how you package that brand to the public via brand name, logos, graphics, advertising, Web site design and content.

5. Yes, you can follow a carefully scripted brand strategy, but if you're not prepared to toss away the script and improvise on the spot, you may never achieve "WOW" in the marketplace.

20

WHEN THE BRAND
SLAM *IS* THE CEO

*"If you want to make good use of your time, you've got to
know what's most important and then give it all you've got."*
Lee Iacocca

In this book's introduction, I said "anything" and "everything" is a brand
and most definitely that includes a company's chief executive officer.
History has shown that many CEOs are a brand slam in and of themselves, and a number of them have been mentioned throughout this book.

One that I would like to introduce now is Jack Welch, CEO of General
Electric Corporation. A *Business Week* article states, "If leadership is an art,
then surely Jack Welch has proven himself a master painter. Few have per-
sonified corporate leadership more dramatically. Few have so consistently
delivered on the results of that leadership. For seventeen years, while big
companies and their chieftains tumbled like dominoes in an unforgiving
global economy, Welch has led to one revenue and earnings record after
another." Under Welch's leadership, GE's market capitalization value has increased from $12 billion in 1981 to $289 billion as of mid-1998. "No one,
not Microsoft's William H. Gates III or Intel's Andrew S. Grove, not Walt
Disney's Michael D. Eisner or Hathaway's Warren E. Buffett, not even the
late Coca-Cola chieftain Roberto C. Goizueta or the late Wal-Mart founder
Sam Walton has created more shareholder value than Jack Welch," according to *Business Week*.[1]

---

1. Source: "How Jack Welch Runs GE" (Business Week, June 8, 1998).

Welch recently received one of the largest nonfiction publishing advances ever—$7 million—to write a business book. Taking into view that Welch is considered by many of Wall Street's movers and shakers to be the CEO of all CEOs in the world, it sounds like a good deal for the publisher. I would be willing to bet that Welch's new book soars to No. 1 on the *New York Times* nonfiction best-seller list the week it's released and that it will remain there for a long time.

According to the *Harvard Business Review,* most company CEOs are colorless. They prefer to stay in the background and make their imprint in the quiet of their suites, by fiat. Yet, the CEOs that I spoke with, some of them featured in this book, expressed their own dynamism and their company's brand slams in a variety of ways.

I must confess that I was expecting to find a "composite CEO type." I found instead that CEOs come in all shapes and sizes—tall, short, husky, and thin. They could be characterized as being shy or outgoing; humorous or dead serious; listeners or talkers; spontaneous or cautious; autocrats or populists; small detailers or broad generalists; and relaxed nine-to-fivers or eighty-hour work addicts.

While there were great differences among them, what hit me with considerable impact was that they all seemed to share these views:

1. They believe in grace, style, and civility. This is evident in themselves and in the people with whom they surround themselves.

2. They feel a commitment to being as good as they can be.

3. They live for challenges and incredible risks.

4. They believe in stirring up apathy—that a noticeable degree of confusion is a healthy sign that "creativity" is in the works.

5. They want to leave a legacy to their corporate heirs or to their industries.

6. They want to make products that they want to own themselves—something better, finer, more beautiful, easier to use, more durable, original, or whatever else that satisfies them.

7. They feel an enormous personal gratitude for being granted the opportunity to work—a chance to make a difference in the world through their businesses.

BRAND SLAMMER LEE IACOCCA

Looking back over the past three decades for an example of a great CEO that was himself a brand slam with the American people, Lee Iacocca leaped to my mind first.

The son of an Italian immigrant, Iacocca was hired as an engineer by Ford Motor Company. He quickly proved that his forte was in sales. By

1960 he had become general manager of the Ford division and a vice president of the company. With his success in launching and promoting the sporty and affordable Ford Mustang, he was named president of Ford in 1970. But his brash and unorthodox style of management finally led to his dismissal in 1978. A year later he was hired by the Chrysler Corporation.

Iacocca literally took up the baton in orchestrating a new life for Chrysler. Taking the helm of a nearly doomed automotive manufacturer, he had no "PT Cruisers" to market. Aside from the best-selling Jeep Cherokee 4x4 and Chrysler's popular Caravan, he inherited a huge inventory of lackluster and mediocre Dodge, Plymouth, and Chrysler brand cars. To make matters worse, they were all low-mileage cars at a time of rising fuel prices. Quite frankly, Iacocca was the only dynamic thing that Detroit's No. 3 carmaker had to offer consumers, and that's what Chrysler advertised.

Fortunately for Chrysler's shareholders, employees, unions, and suppliers, this cigar-smoking CEO was one of the most persuasive brand spokespersons to ever appear in front of a TV camera. As the Iacocca spots aired nationally, it wasn't long before he was considered the most admired chief executive in the land according to a then Gallup poll survey with consumers and leaders in business. In fact, there was a serious grass roots movement building in the nation for Iacocca to run for president of the United States. And one has to believe that Henry Ford II, who fired Iacocca at Ford, had to blink twice each time he saw Iacocca's face on the cover of a leading business magazine. Everyone who worked for him or with him knew he was out to hit more than one brand slam for Chrysler.

"Lee used to phone late at night, and then I'd hear from him first thing in the morning. Two days later, the advertising spot would be on the air. It was fast pace all the time, and it went on for months and months," said Leo Kelmenson, CEO of Kenyon & Eckhart ad agency. "I was on the phone with him at all hours, designing ads . . . evaluating results."

Iacocca worked hard to change the public's perception of Chrysler's products. He authorized the design, engineering, and production of next generation cars and minivans, and built a team of top-notch managers to transform Chrysler into a carmaker to be reckoned with by GM, Ford, Honda, Toyota, and Nissan. He said, "The kind of people I look for to fill top management spots are the eager beavers, the mavericks. These are the guys who try to do more than they're expected to do; they always reach." But it's my opinion that Iacocca put out this charge to his designers, engineers, and production chiefs: "Don't give me strategies, I've got plenty of those. Give me breakaway cars that America wants to buy." And they did exactly that.

Iacocca's business philosophy was simple: We're in this to win! And, like another corporate maverick, Ted Turner, he was known for his cut-to-the-bone sense of humor. One of his best one-liners was, "The trick is to make sure you don't die waiting for prosperity to come."

When he persuaded Congress to bail out Chrysler, he was gambling that it would not allow Chrysler to fail when the national economy was already depressed. Congress in 1980 agreed to guarantee $1.5 billion in loans if the company could raise another $2 billion on its own. Iacocca responded by securing new sources of credit and by trimming operations, closing plants, and convincing labor unions to accept layoffs and wage cuts. He then shifted the company's focus to fuel-efficient cars.

Despite the rough times, Iacocca, gave Chrysler's workers a reason to wake up in the morning and go to work; they could make a difference in their company's products of tomorrow. In his fireside chats to America on national television, he convinced millions of consumers that no other carmaker was more dedicated to building quality products than Chrysler. Iacocca's natural sales ability, along with his guts, determination, and vision of what Chrysler could be helped to catapult the carmaker's flagship brand to highs it hadn't seen in decades. By 1981, Chrysler showed a small profit, and three years later announced record profits of more than $2.4 billion. Iacocca became an international celebrity appearing on TV talk shows. He openly joked in public that had he known it was that easy to borrow money at low interest rates from Uncle Sam, he would have asked for a few billion dollars more. His autobiography *Iacocca* (1984), and his second book, *Talking Straight* (1988), were best-sellers. By the time Iacocca retired as Chrysler's CEO in 1992, he had saved Chrysler and left his heirs a remarkable corporate legacy. Now that's WOW!

All of this underscores the point that taking over an old-economy company or founding a new-economy company is no easy task. The stamina and dynamic of a new organization's leader pulsates throughout the enterprise, however small, extending to all of its important audiences. Others perceive how that leader orchestrates the business and either join that person or not. When they do, the business usually grows. As it grows, it begins to take on a new structure. Meanwhile the leader of the company continues to call the shots, to hire the major players, to work toward improving the company's products or services, and to bring in the talent that can hit brand slams.

A MATTER OF PERSONALITY AND STYLE

No matter how large and complex an organization gets, it usually depends on its success from the decisions made by its chief executive. Throughout the lines of command of any organization—including industry giants—is the vitality pumped by the direct, personal involvement of the CEO. It's his or her policies and qualities that filter downward in the organization and outward to its audiences. In most cases, it is the CEO who infuses the entire operation with a "personality" and "style" that's discernible only to that company; you need only to look at the companies discussed in this book for evidence of that fact.

Yet, it has become a standard practice among industry giants to leave the work of portraying the company's personality and style in the hands of professional corporate image makers. Often CEOs give others the task of wooing the media. That's bad business. The CEO should be a reflection of his or her company.

A Twenty-Four-Hour Job

Experience shows that a CEO's involvement in the day-to-day operations of his or her company can mean the difference between receiving greatness or mediocrity from creative people. Creative people do their best work when the CEO takes personal responsibility for a major brand assignment—giving it the time, attention, and thought it needs and deserves.

What has to change is the distance at which top management and its agencies, brand specialists, product designers, architects, and others, work together. I am referring to the "arm's length" approach, which is too often a preference of CEOs. In short, this approach is not how excellent companies hit brand slams. Among the diverse companies featured in this book, the arm's length approach is never the style of these CEOs. For these companies, specialists in all fields of building a company's brands are treated like confidantes, not hired guns who are not to be trusted by management. The individual at the head of each of these companies is *orchestrating* the action. I use the word "orchestration" because, in a sense, the work of a CEO is very much like that of a conductor who leads and inspires musicians in an orchestra, to bring out the best music possible.

When you're out to hit brand slams, you're open for business twenty-four-hours a day, seven days a week. That's what I tell my clients. If they want to bounce an idea off me in the wee hours of the morning, that's fine with me. I'm probably up working on their brand project anyway. It's funny, only one out of twenty CEOs has ever taken me up on my offer and called me late at night. I guess they're probably sleeping.

Hiring Great Talent

A sports reporter asked Yankees' manager Joe Torre why is it that the New York Yankees hold the record for winning the most World Series Championships? Torre replied, "We hire talented players."

Herman Miller and Bang & Olufsen have this in common: Their most celebrated products are in the permanent collection of the Museum of Modern Art, New York. While Herman Miller's CEO Mike Volkema and

Bang & Olufsen's CEO Anders Knutsen get deeply involved in orchestrating a new product's development, they're smart enough to put the actual product's design in the hands of one of the most talented industrial designers living on planet earth. Therein lies one of their secrets for hitting a brand slam product with consumers.

When IBM's then CEO Thomas Watson, Jr., wanted to score a brand slam corporate identity hit for the computer giant, he hired the renowned graphic designer Paul Rand to execute the company's logo design and company-wide graphic system. When Frito-Lay's top management wanted to communicate more fun and product taste appeal on the package design of its Frito-Lay Doritos, they hired San Francisco-based Landor, a leading package design firm, to refresh the signature chip's logo icon. I think you get the point that hiring great talent will increase your chances of creating WOW in the marketplace. Keep in mind that age, gender, and race have no bearing on the gift of talent.

Since talent is so critical to hitting a brand slam, it amazes me when a company's CEO, after having invested hundreds of millions of dollars in developing a new product, allows the purchasing director to decide who will name the product, design the product, design the product's graphics and packaging, and create the product's advertising. More often than not, these decisions are based solely on cost. In effect, the company sells out to the lowest bidder. Now you know why 90 percent of new products launched in 2000 never got to second base, let alone scored a brand slam hit in the minds of consumers.

LESSONS LEARNED

1. When the product is right, you don't have to be a "spectacular marketer."

2. Make products that you would want to buy for yourself or someone else.

3. The first prerequisite of orchestrating a flagship brand is common sense.

4. Create something great for your customers and you will more than likely succeed.

5. It takes great talent to hit brand slams, but it also takes a CEO with the management vision, courage, and determination to make it happen.

EPILOGUE: BRINGING IT ALL TOGETHER

The message is loud and clear: Toss out that old 300-page strategic brand report and start thinking about how you can greatly surpass your competitors by hitting a brand slam. After all, if there's no big product or service experience idea in that report, it has little value to your company.

Make a list of the practices that everyone in your industry adheres to and identify the ones that annoy your customers the most. Be the first to remove one of these irritants and more than likely you will hit a brand slam with your customers and have your competitors' customers knocking at your door.

Bring back a powerhouse brand name or trademark design from yesteryear that was retired for no logical reason. GM Chevrolet resurrected the Impala brand in 1999 and it hit a PR brand slam with the media. If you don't have any old classics to reinvent, then invent a new brand image that's all your own.

Remember that to get the bases loaded for a shot at hitting a brand slam, you need a great brand name, a great logo design featuring that name, and a great Web site design. This is especially true if you're launching a new company.

Brand names, brand logos, advertising campaigns, brand slogans, package designs, public relations campaigns, Web sites, marriages with other powerhouse brands, new products, and megabrand mergers all offer opportunities to hit brand slams with consumers and other important audiences.

Consumer product brands that remain under the management of caretakers or micro-managers or accounting tacticians run the risk of failing. A big idea that is certain to hit a brand slam with consumers has a way of intimidating brand caretakers because it requires them to bring forth the management vision, courage, determination, and talent to transform that idea into a real-life product or service experience. It doesn't take a marketing genius to manage established brands that are cash cows. But you can ride a cash cow just so long before someone else invents a better mousetrap and then your brand is no longer No. 1 in consumers' minds.

It takes big talent to hit brand slams. Michelangelo was twenty-four-years-old when he sculpted one of his greatest works, "The Rome Pietà." The great Renaissance master needed a "CEO" to fund his next project, and he found him in Cardinal Bilhères de Lagraulas, a Frenchman, who wanted to leave a worthy memorial in his name. So he commissioned Michelangelo to make a Pietà of marble in the round. Little has changed in five centuries; great talent still needs a corporate CEO with the vision, heart, and determination to support and fund a project with brand slam potential.

In the game of baseball, they say "you've gotta swing the bat to hit the ball." In the game of brand slam, you've got to take your best swing at every big idea that comes your way. Walt Disney was sitting on a bench eating peanuts with his two daughters, when he said to himself, "There should be a place where parents and their kids could go to enjoy themselves." Some $17 million later, Disney Land, Disney's first theme park, opened in Anaheim, California, in 1960.

Remember, when you hit a brand slam you not only raise the bar higher for your competitors, your brand takes its place on the world's avenue of the great brand stars.

INDEX